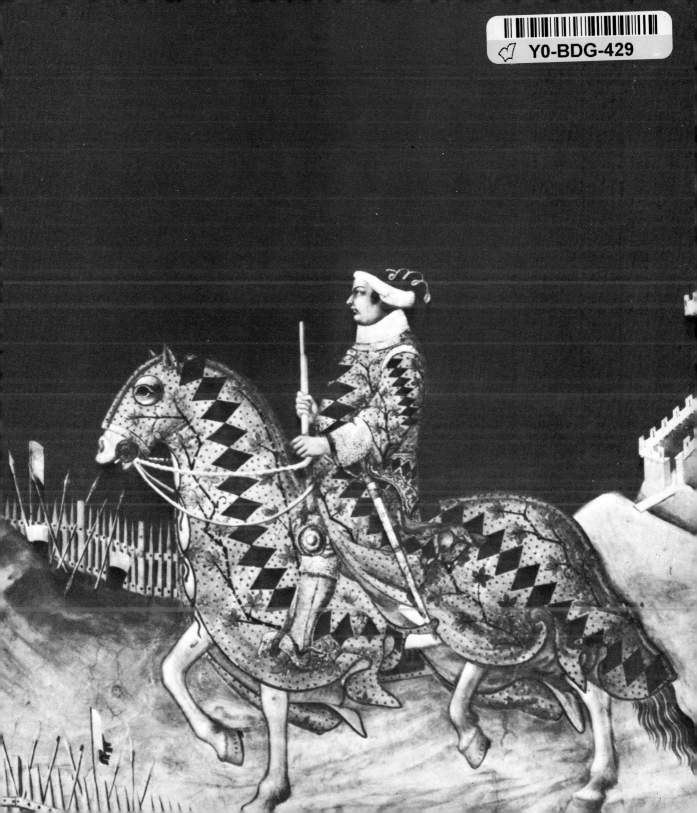

Great Buildings of the World

CASTLES OF EUROPE

by Geoffrey Hindley

PAUL HAMLYN

PUBLISHED BY THE HAMLYN PUBLISHING GROUP LIMITED,
HAMLYN HOUSE, THE CENTRE, FELTHAM, MIDDLESEX

Printed in Great Britain by Fletcher & Son Ltd, Norwich
and bound by Richard Clay (The Chaucer Press) Ltd, Bungay, Suffolk

Endpapers: *Detail of a painting by the 14th-century Sienese artist Simone Martini commemorating the victory by the* **condottiere** *Guidoriccio da Fogliano, here depicted in a fanciful landscape of war.*

Frontispiece: *The Château de Chillon on the shore of Lake Geneva.*

Contents

INTRODUCTION

The subject of this book is twelve great buildings with widely different histories, appearance and even function, yet all commonly called castles. With one exception they were built between 1050 and 1350—the period that saw the birth and maturity of Gothic church architecture. And in a sense, the great bastions of man such as Krak des Chevaliers are the secular parallels of the great cathedrals, which were regarded as the bastions of God in a sinful world. In some parts of Europe, churches were even built to look like castles. The most famous of these fortress churches, as they are called, is the cathedral of Albi in the south of France; and often, as at Avila, the apse of a church projecting through the fortifications served as an additional tower on the walls.

In one way, then, this book is about medieval secular architecture, though it is secular architecture of a particular kind. The word castle has a wide meaning, since it may apply equally to a single stone tower or to an enclosure and complex of buildings covering several thousand square feet. The idea of walled fortifications was not an invention of the middle ages; the walls of Babylon were one of the seven wonders of the ancient world, and recent excavations show that the walls of Biblical Jericho are almost as old as civilisation itself. In Europe, the fortified city has a long span of development, lasting from the formidable prehistoric earthworks of Mai Dun castle in Dorset to the third-century masonry walls of Aurelian at Rome and reaching its peak in the great line of walls built in the early fifth century by Theodosius II at Constantinople. The walled city was the bulwark of civilisation from its earliest beginnings, and continued as a feature of the European scene until the development of gunpowder and artillery made it obsolete. Perhaps the most famous

Opposite, a detail from a 15th-century representation of a castle under siege.

Opposite, the cathedral at Albi (begun 1282), whose massive tower looks more like the turreted keep of a castle. The thick walls and narrow windows reinforce the fortress-like impression. The interior, a simple nave without aisles, has a similarly workmanlike appearance.

The walls at Avila (left) are still intact, and provide a classic example of the kind of walled town found all over medieval Europe.

Above, part of the great walls of Constantinople begun under Theodosius II (408–50). These historic walls, girdling the greatest city of the middle ages, stood unbreached for 1000 years until they finally fell to the Turks in 1453.

Left, Mai Dun (often called Maiden Castle) in Dorset—a Celtic variant of the walled town. The hillside falling away on all sides has been sculpted into a number of obstacles and the main entrance, to the right, offers a series of 'breakwaters' against the incoming tide of an attack.

surviving example is the much restored cité at Carcassone in the south of France, but many of the towns of Europe must have had a similar appearance as the bastions of property and commerce facing a hostile world of marauding armies and lawless aristocrats.

But as well as continuing to build walled cities, medieval military architects also produced something new. This was the fortified residence, built by a rich and powerful man, which is the origin of the military strongpoint we call the castle. As we shall see, during the three hundred years reviewed in this study, the castle developed from simple stone towers and wooden fortifications into fortresses of immense complexity. But as well as differences in style, the castles of Europe present us with a rich and romantic diversity of site and function, ranging from the lonely border stronghold of Hermitage, near Roxburgh in Scotland, to the island site of Sidon in the Levant. A castle might be the refuge of a great lord and his dependants from the incursions of invading Norsemen; it might be the stronghold of a

Above, the cité at Carcassonne, built under Louis IX and Philip the Bold of France during the 13th century and restored under Viollet-le-Duc during the 19th.

13

garrison in a hostile territory such as England after the Norman conquest; it might be the headquarters used by a powerful and lawless leader for launching his depredations on the surrounding neighbourhood; or it might, like the Edwardian castles of Wales and, to a lesser extent, the crusader castles in Syria, be part of a strategic system. A garrison could control a civil population within a fair radius of its walls, but if the land was invaded by a hostile army, a castle could play only a limited role: that of a potential threat to the enemy lines of communication and a possible point of concentration for the defending forces. We must be careful of talking too glibly of a castle 'commanding' a pass or 'controlling' a vital route. Such terms could only be applied in times of peace. In war the advance of a hostile army would engulf the castle as completely as an incoming tide does a rock. The garrison would then be powerless to prevent the plundering of the surrounding country and to halt the enemy advance. Yet if the invaders were determined on outright conquest, then the castles had to be captured; otherwise they would be possible pockets of resistance and a danger to the communications of the invading army. In this way the crusader castles made an important contribution to the persistence of the Latin states in the Levant; as long as they remained in Christian hands, the local populations could once more be brought under Christian rule.

The ruins of the crusader castle at Sidon. Built on a sandbank just off the coast, this little fortress used the sea itself for a moat.

Life in the castle

The castles of Europe are steeped in history and those reviewed in this book are no exception. Yet in many of the twelve chapters that follow, we shall find that the century from the 1170s to the 1270s in particular was crammed with important events that affected not only the physical shape of the fortresses but their role in political affairs. And as our study progresses, we shall be struck by the number of direct personal and political ties linking the various families that built or ruled in the various buildings; it may therefore be worth taking a brief look at some of these connections.

The 13th century saw the decline of two great institutions of the earlier middle ages—the crusades and the Empire—and the consolidation of the two major royal houses in Western Europe—those of France and England—and the lands belonging to them. The process was long drawn out, yet, except for a few later repercussions, by

The encounter between Richard II of England and the usurper Henry of Lancaster (later Henry IV) at the castle of Flint (from an early 15th-century manuscript).

15

the reigns of Louis IX in France and of Henry III in England, we can begin to make out the outlines of a pattern that was to dominate the internal affairs of both countries. Although the Third Crusade, Christendom's last great venture to the Holy Land, made allies of the two bitter rivals, Richard the Lionheart of England and Philip Augustus of France, conflict between them over the extensive English holdings in France was inevitable. This struggle came to a head outside the walls of Château Gaillard, built by Richard as a vital part of the defence of his Norman possessions. Its capture in 1204 from his brother King John meant the loss of Normandy, while the loss of the county of Anjou to the French was marked by the building of the great castle at Angers by Philip's grandson Louis IX. The ambitions of Louis's brother Charles, who had received Anjou, added to papal support led to a French involvement in the south of Italy (formerly ruled by the Emperor Frederick II, lord of Castel del Monte) that was to continue for another two centuries.

Henry of England, too, had at one time had interests in the Sicilian venture; he was also linked to Charles by marriage: both 16 had married daughters of Count Berenger of Provence and were

Above, a ceremonial banquet in a castle at which the King of Portugal entertains John of Gaunt (from a late 15th-century manuscript).

Right, the Duke of Berry dines in state in one of his castles; in the background the tapestries depict scenes of knightly combat before a fortress. The duke was a renowned patron of the arts, and this painting depicting the month of January comes from his famous book of hours Les Très Riches Heures du Duc de Berri.

Below, the French royal palace of Vincennes rises up beyond the trees in this winter hunting scene from Les Très Riches Heures; *note the numerous towers and the great keep.*

thus brothers-in-law. This marriage, however, brought Henry into more direct contact with the continent, since his wife's family arrived in England to exploit her new position. One of the noblest of these adventurers was Peter II of Savoy, who was largely responsible for the final shape of the castle at Chillon. Finally, as a result of the Savoyard connection, Edward I employed a Savoyard architect James St George, to design the fortresses of North Wales.

When visiting the sites of these great castles, now often little more than ruins, it is easy to forget that they were first built for a specific purpose. A castle might, like Pevensey, be the residence of a great feudal lord, or, like Vincennes in France, of the king himself. But every castle of moderate size would house a considerable number of people, and as the middle ages progressed, the accommodation became increasingly specialised and complex. The basic requirements were a great hall, a separate chamber for the lord and his family and ample storage space. In a very primitive castle, the hall would not only serve as a central refectory where special banquets were held and as a hall of justice, but would also accommodate the large proportion of the garrison that was without quarters in the wooden outbuildings inside the stockade. As well as living quarters for servants and soldiers, these outbuildings would include kitchens, stables, mews and additional storage space for food and fodder. In a large castle, accommodation in the fortress itself would be on a much more lavish scale, even though the inner courtyard might still contain a number of timber buildings. Rooms would have to be provided for the lord himself and his family, and these might include a separate great hall for their personal use; a further suite of rooms also with a separate hall would make up the state apartments, while yet another suite might be set aside for visitors of a less exalted rank than those privileged to use the state rooms. And as well as these great rooms, space would of course have to be provided for the officials, soldiers and staff. The establishment of a large fortress might number about 300 in peacetime, while the full wartime complement of a major crusader castle like Beaufort might be as much as 2000.

More often than not the lord of the castle himself would be absent. He might be fighting for the king, attending the royal court, on a crusade in the Holy Land, or visiting other parts of his honour (as a great feudal barony was called). In his absence, the castle would be in the charge of his lady or of the castellan, and it is worth remarking in passing that the great ladies of the middle ages often exercised considerable authority. The management of a household

Like this great banqueting hall at Bunratty Castle in Ireland with its magnificent timber roof, the great hall of a castle was often on the first floor.

19

of a 100 or more people called for a great deal of administrative skill, and occasionally the châtelaine might find herelf in command of the castle's military strength, as when the stout old Lady Nicolaa de la Haye held Lincoln for the king's party during the civil wars in England after the death of King John.

Since a castle was primarily built for war, it always had to be kept in a state of readiness, even when times were peaceful and untroubled. Without a continual flow of fresh supplies, a fortress was defenceless, so that provisions had to be kept up to a wartime level throughout the year and the barrels opened in rotation. If a lazy cook were allowed always to take his daily requirements from the most conveniently placed bins—for example, those nearest the door—half the rations might be found to be putrid and inedible when the castle was unexpectedly attacked. Daily watch had also to be kept on the well or spring within the keep to see that the water remained sweet and free from decaying rubbish thrown out by careless kitchen staff. The defences of the castle had to be kept in good repair, and the garrison well drilled; in troubled times, the drawbridge was kept raised but was lowered promptly and rapidly to admit friends. Other daily responsibilities of the castellan, or lord's deputy in charge of the castle, might include seeing that the horses were well groomed or that the walls of the keep were kept free of flammable fodder piled against them with the connivance of a lazy bailiff; he would also supervise the servants and officials so that the community functioned smoothly from day to day. The chief officers of the castle were the castellan, the constable, the butler and the steward; below them were a floating contingent of knights. (Many of the knights might hold land in the surrounding countryside by tenure of castle guard, which obliged them serve for forty days a year within the castle walls.) Next in seniority were the lesser clerks, some with administrative posts, others serving the chapel or chapels of the fortress; more junior still were the lesser officers of the military establishment and professionals such as the armourer, the head groom, the farrier, the falconer and the chief huntsman; at the bottom of the ladder were the simple sergeants and crossbowmen, often mercenaries and foreigners, yet, as fighting men, ranking above the scullions and kitchen staff. These groups formed a complex community, but one which was predominantly male; the womenfolk of the high-ranking officers might live inside the castle, but those of the lower orders would be housed either in the timber buildings of the outer enceinte or, more probably, in the township adjoining the fortress.

Although much restored, the castle kitchen and its great fireplace (above) at Marksburg in Germany must have looked much like this in medieval times.

Opposite, the spacious well-lit hall at Nuremberg, which, like that of Bunratty, was on the first floor.

21

The building and the builders

Sooner or later, the visitor to any of the great sites described in this book will ask himself how they came to be built: not only who designed and conceived the castles themselves, but how the building operation was actually organised. The castles and cathedrals of Europe are today often an integral part of the townships that have grown up around them and it is not always easy to realise that at one stage the site was wild countryside or perhaps occupied by utterly different structures. These great buildings involved the mobilisation of huge supplies of materials and manpower, as well as the exercise of great imagination and professional talent. So to give some idea of the whole operation, we shall now explain in some detail how a 22 great fortress was built, concentrating on castles in England and

Above, a representation (from a 13th-century manuscript) of water being fetched from the well and wine from the cellar.

Window seats like this at Chinon (right) are found in many castles and must have been favourite haunts of the châtelaine and her ladies.

Wales, where the researches of scholars such as Professor Goronwy Edwards and Mr John Harvey have provided the student with much detailed knowledge of the builders and their methods.

The decision to build of course originated with the ruler or great landowner. The choice of a site was crucially important, since the position of the castle largely determined its efficiency as a fighting unit. Ideally, the site should be a natural strongpoint, on a rocky eminence or near a river or stream that could be diverted to supply the moat and to provide access by water for bringing in relief forces and supplies. The castle should also be so sited that the garrison was not only well protected against attack, but also able to control a strategic point such as an important mountain pass, a major city or a vital waterway. A castle's position was also important for another reason, as we shall now see.

Even in peacetime, it was the centre of a thriving community, very often housing the administrative officials of the district and requiring some kind of standing garrison no matter how small; further it needed constant maintenance. The periodic scraping of the moat, the repairs to roofs or the servicing of the fortifications themselves cost money in labour and materials. So as well as the immense building costs, which often had to be discharged initially by the central exchequer, the running costs had to be met as far as

Above, a royal or noble client is shown over the castle site by the master-mason. A tower is under construction, scaffolding is being erected and a windlass and pulley block and tackle being used to raise the stone (from a 15th-century Flemish book of hours).

The bricklayers using plumb lines and levels on the walls and the mason shaping the column in the foreground of this 13th-century miniature, left, would have been among the skilled (and more highly paid) labourers.

24

possible out of local resources. The builder therefore had to consider whether the surrounding country could in fact support the expenses of the place. In the Levant this was a particularly important consideration. A mighty fortress like Krak not only was a superb natural strongpoint, well placed strategically, but it also overlooked rich farm lands to the east. One pilgrim described the castles of Outremer as set among well-stocked fields and vegetable gardens and surrounded by orchards and farmsteads. In Europe, the problem was usually different. The surrounding lands, if not cultivated already, were likely to be potentially fertile; but they were also likely to be owned or controlled by someone else. At Château Gaillard the site belonged to the Church—an opponent whom even Richard the Lionheart had to placate eventually. Disputes could also arise involving jurisdiction over the castle's inmates and the surrounding population; the right

Religion was a central part of medieval life and every castle had a chapel, which, like that at Nuremberg Castle, above, was often extremely handsome.

to maintain a castle chapel might also be disputed by the local ecclesiastical authorities. These points are made to emphasise the impact of a new castle in the local community, quite apart from its possible effect on the military map of the district.

Once a site was selected, the actual work of building began. Both men and materials had to be mustered in huge quantities: no fewer than 970 men were engaged on the works at Caernarvon during the summer season of 1285, while at the same time, intensive work was going forward at Conway and Harlech. Altogether these castles absorbed a working force of some 2500 men during that one year alone. The work demanded a wide variety of skilled and semi-skilled labour. At Harlech in the following year, documents record payments to a weekly average labour force of about 170 masons, 90 quarriers, 28 carpenters, 24 smiths, 520 unskilled labourers and some 26 administrative staff. These workmen came from every shire's end of England, not only from neighbouring counties adjoining Wales such as Gloucester and Cheshire but from as far afield as Northumberland and Essex. In 1277, 300 fossatores, or navvies, were sent from Hoyland in Yorkshire to the works at Flint and Rhuddlan.

During the last quarter of the 13th century, local officials throughout England were involved in the huge administrative operation needed to complete the chain of strategic fortresses that King Edward threw around the intractable heart of the Welsh rebellion. Sheriffs were ordered to supply both men and materials just as some fifty years earlier the sheriff of London had been ordered to supply Master Thomas the Carpenter and Nicholas his mate with firwood for the doors and windows of the king's new castle at Nottingham. Although the workmen were often pressed into service, they received day wages. Here again the sheriff's responsibility was a heavy one, since it was often his duty to supply the labourer's pay during his journey from his home county to the castle site. As today, labour costs represented the largest item of the total expense—about two-thirds as far as can be deduced from the records.

Since the workmen were often forced into service, they could not always be relied on. The wastage rate by desertion could be serious if no precautions were taken. The payroll for Rhuddlan mentions three horsemen, whose job it was to guard the navvies from Yorkshire, and they could hardly have been unique. Other forms of discipline, such as the fines levied for breaches of conduct, were enforced by courts, sometimes presided over by the clerk of the works or the chief mason on the site. Walter of Hereford, who was in charge of

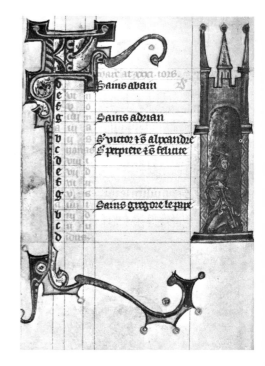

Building a castle involved shifting a mass of earth. Fossatores (or navvies), like the one shown in the late 13th-century miniature, above, were employed in hundreds for this work.

Reducing the timber to planks was the specialised job of sawyers, here depicted (above) in the border illustration to a 12th-century manuscript.

Left, carpenters at work shaping wood and planing it with adzes (from a late 13th-century manuscript).

the works at Caernarvon, was allowed to hold a free court to try workmen on the site in the year 1295. The fines were paid to him and may have formed quite a valuable perquisite. There must have been considerable scope for graft and extortion, and one can only hope that the chief master-mason was a man of honour.

The labourers' lot seems to have been unenviable. Forced to exchange their homes and ordinary occupations for rough encampments in a remote and rebellious country, they were also submitted to rigorous discipline, and must have looked forward eagerly to the end of the building season in November when they were free to return home until the following April. We can only glean a few hints of their life, but the careers of their superiors are better documented and so it is to them we now turn.

Men like James St George, the Savoyard master-mason who seems to have been in general charge of the Welsh castle-building programme, Walter Hereford or Richard Lenginour, probably the principal architect of the castle and town of Conway, had reached the top of their profession and enjoyed considerable salaries and status. By 1293 St George's annual fees from various sources amounted to 100 marks or £66 13s. 4d.; the modern equivalent might be as much as £6000 a year, but we get a better idea of the real value if we compare it with the cost of the great hall and royal apartments at Conway, which were built for £100. St George also seems to have been a personal friend of the king and from 1284 onwards was provided with a pension of three shillings a day for life or, after his death, of one shilling and sixpence to be paid to his widow. With the pension went the title of 'king's serjeant', but a rather more meaningful appointment, which he took up in the same year, was his position as keeper of the works at Conway—a post that involved the administration of £6000 in building expenditure. In July 1290, he was appointed Constable of Harlech—a distinguished achievement for a man who began life as a skilled artisan. But St George's successful career was not an isolated example; in the next century, we find William de Ramsey, chief surveyor of the king's works in the Tower of London and other castles south of the River Trent, assessed for a contribution of £10 towards the city of London's forced loan to King Edward III in 1340; he too appears to have been not only a man of wealth but to have climbed some way up the social ladder, since we know that his seal carried arms.

The chief architects and master-masons could earn this kind of high reward, yet even the ordinary labourer might receive a bonus—

Opposite, a 15th-century representation of the building of the Tower of Babel showing some of the techniques and equipment available to medieval builders including pulleys and a horse with panniers to transport the stone; in the foreground masons can be seen dressing the stone.

Left, another example of a windlass and pulley (from a 13th-century French manuscript).

e dono regis, 'by the King's gift'—for work well done. Certainly in the building of the Edwardian castles of Wales (and, one assumes, in the building of any great fortress), the main object was speed. It was said that Richard I's Château Gaillard took only one year to build—an exaggerated claim although even the more probable estimate of three years represents a fantastic achievement. We know for sure, however, that at Conway the 1400 yards of curtain wall, 30 feet high, its protective ditch, 22 towers and three gates were completed in the period 1283 to 1287. This represents a total time of 40 months since building operations only took place between April and November.

Before work could begin, the site might have to be cleared either to make way for the new fortress or to improve its defensive position by removing any form of cover surrounding the area. At Caernarvon some of the houses of the little Welsh township had to be demolished

to make way for the great walls, while James St George, directing operations at Rhuddlan, was ordered to uproot the king's woods surrounding the castle. After such preliminary work, the line of the moat or ditch was marked out and the excavation begun. At this stage too, the whole site was enclosed in a temporary wooden palisade to protect the works from raids by rebellious locals. Next, the foundations of the main curtain wall were laid and the wall itself and its towers were built up to a reasonable height; the full circuit of the battlements and wall-walks were completed later. The main

A 15th-century miniature showing a castle's wall and tower in the final stages of completion. Often, as shown here, the scaffolding of a tower would be supported on beams projecting from the finished masonry.

31

residential quarters, usually timber-framed houses inside the main courtyard, would be among the last buildings to go up, unless (as at Caernarvon) temporary accommodation had to be provided for the king and his household when he came to inspect the works. It was at this stage that Simon the Glazier of Chester, for example, was commissioned to provide nine glass windows for the royal chambers and that Richard Lenginour and Henry of Oxford accepted the contract to build the halls and chambers at Conway.

It is difficult to give an accurate estimate of the cost of these great works, because the records, although full, do not record all the details necessary for a full picture of the pattern of expenditure. It is also hard (as we have seen) to find any meaningful way of comparing the value of money. Goronwy Edwards has estimated the total cost of Caernarvon to have been about £16,000, that of Conway £19,000 and the total for all the Welsh castles to have amounted to £80,000. This is a huge figure in medieval terms, and it seems fairly certain that it contributed considerably to the strained state of the royal finances that led to the constitutional crisis of 1296.

A master-mason receives instructions from his royal patron. Again note the scaffolding supported by beams projecting from the masonry. (At Conway Castle these post holes can be clearly seen spiralling up around the towers.)

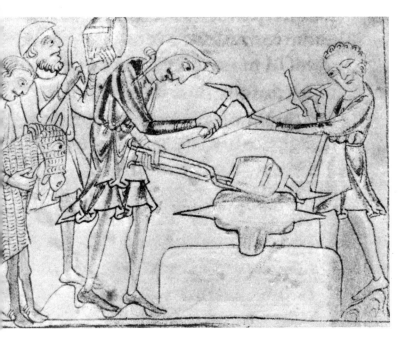

A 13th-century representation of armourers at work; one is working a helmet on the anvil, the other aligns the blade of a sword before fixing on the handle.

The castle at war

The embattled fortress under siege is the picture that first comes to mind when one thinks of the medieval castle but, as we have seen, the castle also played a major part in the daily life of the district. Even so, the fortresses of medieval Europe were shaped by military considerations and a state of siege was, so to speak, their natural element. This section, therefore, is concerned with the castle's defences and the weapons and techniques employed by its defenders and attackers. Obviously, castles differed from period to period and from place to place; they might be complicated or simple, of major or of minor strategic importance, but to get as full a picture as possible of siege warfare we shall take as examples major fortifications such as Krak, Conway or Château Gaillard.

There were certain features common to all castles that determined how smoothly they could be run and how long they could withstand attack. First, the castle had to be built with an eye to the strength of the potential enemy. For example, many of the great Byzantine fortresses were built in a country where the people were comparatively unsophisticated in the science of war and there was little danger of attack with heavy siege engines. Consequently, although precautions were taken to protect the main walls from capture by escalade or from being undermined, the walls themselves could be comparatively thin by later standards. The walls of the great crusader bastions in Syria on the other hand, which had to withstand attack from an enemy versed in every subtlety of the siege and armed with powerful artillery, were immensely thick and strong. Secondly, for the castle to be fully effective, the garrison had to be up to strength, so that the full circuit of walls and towers could be properly manned and the designers' arrangements fully exploited. In fact, available manpower would be an extremely important factor in the design of the castle itself. And here again the situation in the Levant provides an illuminating contrast. The castles of Justinian and the Byzantine rulers were designed at a time when manpower was plentiful. As a result, many of the Byzantine castles look more like walled camps, or ancient Roman *castra*, than castles in the sense understood by their crusader successors. The crusaders were continually plagued by a shortage of human material, and for this reason they designed defence works that were powerful enough to be defended by small or depleted garrisons. Thirdly, the garrison, however small, had to be well provisioned both with food and water and with ammunition. The well inside the walls was an essential part of the defensive system and was usually reinforced by open rainwater cisterns on the walls, as at Caernarvon. Storage space for supplies and weapons was in the wall towers or in cellars or undercrofts as at Krak or the Gravensteen at Ghent. The fourth and last factor that determined a castle's defensive capacity was the morale of the garrison. Since the garrison's situation itself undermined their attacking spirit, the sortie, besides disconcerting the attackers, was of major psychological importance. However slight the gains of an attack beyond the walls, the chance it gave for displaying knightly prowess or physical bravery, for embittered retaliation, or for mere exercise was likely to raise, if only temporarily, the spirits of the whole garrison. The more effectively the fortress was sealed off from the outside world, the more likely it was that rumour and despondency inside the walls would do the attackers' work for them. As the middle ages progressed, the military architect's skill developed to a point where a great castle was almost impregnable; the imponderables of morale therefore played an increasingly important role in deciding the outcome.

To sum up then, the four factors governing the castle's ability to withstand siege were its successful adaptation to its hostile environ-

Above, the main well at the Wartburg. Here it is in the main courtyard, but often it would have been inside the keep itself.

Right, the castle on the rocca maggiore *at Assisi—a good example of a well-chosen site; note the town wall stretching up the hillside.*

35

ment; the availability of manpower; the state of the supplies and the morale of the garrison. Even the most complex fortifications were useless if any one of these conditions was not fulfilled. Having emphasised that point, we now turn our attention to the castle's actual defences. All good castle architecture, from the simplest to the most complicated, is based on a correct appraisal of the site itself. Even the mighty Krak derives its basic form from the contours of the spur of rock on which it is built. The aim of the castle builder is to hold a position against military attack, and he achieves this aim by presenting the attacking forces with a series of obstacles. If he does his job well, he exploits the features of the ground that contribute to his purpose and where nature offers no help, he uses his ingenuity. Except in the most primitive fortifications the first obstacle is the wall; yet even the highest walls can be scaled and even the thickest walls must have an entrance. If the approach to the wall

Far left, a view of the casemates in one of the surviving walls of the crusader castle of El Kerak showing the arrow loops from the inside.

Left, the ornate battlements of Palazzo Vecchio in Florence, most of which was built in the early 14th century.

Opposite, the castle at Bodiam, built in the late 14th century by Sir Edward Dalyngrygg. It is entirely surrounded by a moat and every inch of the curtain wall could be covered by weapons fired from the projecting towers. It was built to repel French pirate marauders of the Channel ports but may also have been something of an old soldier's dream castle.

37

was not already impeded by a steep slope, a dry ditch or a water-filled moat would be dug out to form an artificial obstacle. (This was often a hazard to health as well as to life, since the latrines of the castle usually discharged into it.) Later, as the skill of the military architect advanced, walls came to be protected not only by outworks of this kind, but by towers projecting from the main line of the fortifications. These provided the defenders with a commanding position from which they could fire down on the enemy soldiers who had successfully reached the foot of the walls. The attackers then had to face the concentrated fire from the battlements above them, from the loopholes in the main wall itself and the battlements and loopholes of the towers projecting on either side. From outside, these arrow loops appeared as narrow slits, but inside the wall the slit splayed out on each side so that the archers (probably crossbowmen) could direct their fire in a wide lateral arc. The crossbow was at a disadvantage on the open field of battle, since the loading of the bolt was a slow operation that needed the archer's full attention; the longbow, favoured by the English, proved to be a superior infantry weapon because of its firing speed—about five times greater than that of its rival. Yet the crossbow fired a heavier projectile with considerably more force. Consequently the crossbow was preferred for siege warfare where the defenders were protected by the battlements and the attackers made use of heavy shields, or pavises, set in the ground. Obviously men on the walls were less well protected than those inside them. The soldier on the battlements had to leave the safety of the merlon (the rising member of the battlement) to fire over the lower retaining wall of the embrasure; from the late 12th century onwards, however, embrasures were provided with wooden shutters, which protected the bowmen even when opened outwards to allow for firing. Further refinements, such as the multiple arrow loops at Caernarvon for the release of simultaneous crossfire from the same point in the wall, made it possible to produce a truly murderous concentration of firepower.

But if the castle were to be won by assault, the walls had to be breached or scaled. If scaling was impossible, the attackers were obliged to undermine the masonry of the wall itself. At this stage they would be bombarded with a shower of missiles ranging from rocks to the legendary boiling oil, which were dropped directly on to them from a wooden hoarding, or brattice, projecting from the line of the battlements. A brattice was a temporary structure supported on wooden beams, slotted into sockets left in the masonry. Planks were

laid across the beams with gaps left at intervals and the whole structure was protected by a wooden penthouse roof. But since it was made of wood, the brattice was obviously vulnerable to fire—a major weapon in the medieval armoury. Designers therefore came to prefer a stone version supported on corbels, which was a permanent part of the fabric. A very early example of the stone brattice—more correctly called a machicolation—may have been used at Château Gaillard, where the buttresses around the keep may have been intended to support such a structure. Certainly, the projecting corbels over the main entrance to Conway originally carried a machicolation.

These were the precautions taken to protect the solid stonework of the curtain wall. Around the main entrance gate, the works were even more complicated and intimidating. The gateway was, after all, a ready-made breach in the wall, and even in the earliest castles it was defended with the greatest possible ingenuity. In early stone towers, such as the White Tower at London, the south tower of the Wartburg and many others, the entrance to the building was above ground level and was approached by an external stairway. At Rochester, the foot of this stair and the entrance to which it leads are sited on two different walls, so that the attackers had to negotiate an exposed right-angled turn under the fire of the defending force. Another device was to enclose the approach stair in an outwork fitted with arrow loops and the usual repertoire of defensive devices.

An entrance in an outside wall posed a rather different problem—because of its position at ground level. The approach across the ditch or moat was usually by way of a wooden bridge, which could be raised against the gateway, so forming an additional door. There were two types of mechanism for raising the bridge: the drawbridge in which the wooden roadway, hinged at one end, was raised by chains, or the swing bridge in which the roadway was balanced by counterweights free to pivot in a well behind the gate. But the gate itself was always vulnerable and difficult to defend. Since the sorties sometimes launched from the main gate had to return through it, it was essential that the entrance should be closed as soon as possible to prevent the attackers from following the returning garrison back into the enceinte. A barrier worked by gravity, which could rattle down almost immediately, was therefore an obvious advance over a gate that had to be laboriously manhandled into position. The portcullis, a strong wooden lattice structure shod with iron spikes, 40 was a barrier of this type, and became a regular feature in many

The crossbowman's vulnerability while loading was lessened by the use of protective shields or pavises, here depicted in a 15th-century miniature.

great fortresses. But wood, however scientifically used, was still too vulnerable, and so the main gatehouse became the centre of an elaborate system of machicolations and arrow loops that subjected the attackers to a crossfire that was even more intense than that they had to meet on the curtain wall. But even this was sometimes felt to be an inadequate way of defending this dangerously weak point in the defences of the castle. In castle after castle, more and more powerful and complex systems of counterattack were developed. At the Gravensteen, the gatehouse was raised to the status of a little outer castle. At Caernarvon, extra portcullises and drawbridges were built into the structure; in addition, a right-angled turn compelled the attackers to follow the murder route dictated by the garrison, while at the great castle of Krak the attackers were offered a choice between a death trap extending up a steep slope covered by machicolations

The walls of the castle on the rocca maggiore *at Assisi, showing battering at the base of the towers, deep battlements on the projecting round tower and stone corbels, which originally carried machicolations.*

Left, the keep at Rochester clearly showing the first-floor entrance commonly found in early stone castles. On the left is the forebuilding enclosing part of the approach stair, which rises from the foot of the tower (here partly obscured by a tree).

Below, the elaborate main entrance to the great 13th-century castle at Aleppo.

and unexpected sally points for the defenders or entry into the inner bailey between the crossfire from the inner and outer walls.

Castle defence centred on two crucial points: the outer curtain wall, which was the first line of opposition, and the entrance, the weakest point of the whole system. In an attempt to postpone the awful moment of defeat and capture, the designers of the great defensive fortresses of Europe and the Levant developed the system known as the concentric castle. One of the earliest examples is to be found in France at the magnificent Château Gaillard, the astonishing fortification built by Richard the Lionheart, the hero of the Third Crusade. Basically, the concentric fortress consisted of a courtyard surrounded by two curtain walls; it was a popular form of design among the Knights Hospitaller, who used it for their castles in the Levant, and it may be that its adoption in Europe was prompted by the experiences of the returning crusaders. Nevertheless, it is worth pointing out that Château Gaillard antedates the greatest example of the concentric castle in the Middle East—Krak—by about ten years.

From the defence of the castle we turn now to its attack. As we have seen, the attackers' morale was probably higher, but obviously psychology did not—and does not—win battles outright. How else could the besiegers gain an advantage? By the cat, by the mine, by starvation. By the belfry, by assault. By cunning, by force.

The most straightforward, but also the most laborious, method of reducing an obdurate garrison was by starvation—by surrounding the fortress with an impenetrable line of counterdefences that prevented any attempt at a sortie by the defenders from inside or any efforts to relieve them from outside. At the siege of Château Gaillard, the French King Philip Augustus built a double trench that entirely cut off the garrison in the hope of either starving them into surrender, or at least of persuading them that all attempts at defence were doomed. He was foiled in both aims, but the technique was used often enough. The next stage was the assault, and for this to be successful the attacker first had to make a breach in the walls of the fortress.

The wall could be brought down either by mining operations at its foot or at long range by various forms of artillery. No examples of these siege engines survive, but from descriptions we can form a fairly full idea of the main types. They were the balista, the trebuchet and the mangonel. The first was in effect a gigantic crossbow, and fired heavy bolts similar to those of the hand weapon. The other two threw stones and were sometimes generically referred to as petrariae. The trebuchet consisted of a long, wooden pole, weighted at one end,

Opposite, part of a 14th-century French tapestry of the siege of Jerusalem by the Emperor Titus depicts a sortie hard pressed as it returns under the portcullis of the main gate.

Above left, the drawbridge at the Wartburg, which was approached by a narrow winding path.

Below left, the portcullis mechanism above the gate leading to the Bloody Tower in the Tower of London.

the lower part of which pivoted on an axle. At the free end, there was a leather pouch or sling for holding the stone or stones; to fire the engine, the free end of the pole was forced into a horizontal position against the pull of the counterweight and secured with ropes. The sling was then loaded and the ropes cut so that the pole swung violently up as the counterweight fell back to its original position, hurling the stone in a high curve over the castle walls. The mangonel had a somewhat flatter trajectory and could be used for bombarding the walls. The impetus was provided by torque. A timber beam, hollowed at one end to take the projectile, was held at its base between cords of twisted rope, which turned it in a vertical arc when the beam was released. The beam was kept vertical by a stop and the projectile was flung forward horizontally. Siege engines were also used for throwing fire balls at, for example, the brattices or into the inner castle or town in the hope of starting a general blaze; or they might hurl the bodies of prisoners captured in a sortie back into the castle to demoralise the garrison. At the siege of the town of Caffa on the Black Sea in the 1340s, the Mongol commander ordered the bodies of plague victims to be thrown over the walls in what must be one of the earliest examples of biological warfare. After the town's capture the inhabitants were sold into slavery. Some reached the slave markets of Italy and it has been suggested that it was they who brought the Black Death to Europe.

Besides this long-range bombardment, the wall might be undermined or sapped or an attempt might be made to scale it. In either case, the first move was to build a causeway over the ditch or moat by filling in part of it with soil and rubble. Since this work had to be carried out under fire from the garrison, it often meant considerable loss of life for the attacking forces. Various ways were thought of for lessening the danger, all of which consisted basically of a wooden penthouse roofing. This might be built out to form a corridor running from the attackers' lines to the edge of the moat or it might be built on wheels so that it could gradually be moved across the causeway as it grew. The cat, as it was called, was used in the final stages of the siege of Château Gaillard in the attack on the inner bailey. Once the sappers had made their way to the walls under the hail of missiles, they would attack them either with a battering ram or by sapping or by mining.

The battering ram, one of the oldest (and one of the least efficient) weapons, was a heavy wooden beam, shod with iron at one end. It was slung from the framework of the penthouse roof, under which

A 15th-century drawing showing the English army besieging Rouen; note that the town's drawbridge is firmly raised.

47

Left, a 14th-century representation of a siege at a point of crisis; an attack is being launched on the main gate to the left, sappers are at work and scaling ladders are up at three points.

Below left, an early 14th-century miniature showing a trebuchet being prepared for firing.

Below, an early 15th-century Florentine painted panel provides an elegant panorama of the bloody business of siege warfare.

This fine illumination from a 13th-century manuscript, left, shows another type of trebuchet with a different type of counterweight mechanism to that shown on the opposite page.

Below, an elaborate type of ballista or arblet designed by Leonardo da Vinci.

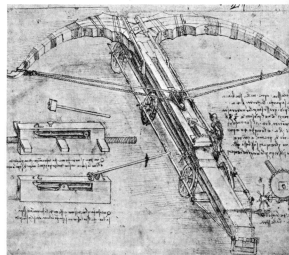

49

the soldiers swung it against the wall or the gate under attack. The ram's drawbacks were its slowness and the number of counter-measures that could be used against it. One of these was a fender of straw and hides, which could be lowered to absorb the shock; another was a forked instrument for grappling with the ram, which was operated from the battlements. Whereas the ram tried to batter the wall down, sapping involved tearing out the lower courses of the masonry so that the wall collapsed. But of all the methods of attacking the walls and towers of the castle, mining was by far the most lethal. First the miners dug the soil away from under the foundations, which they then shored up with wooden props as the work proceeded. When a large enough area of wall had been undermined, the wooden props were fired and, as the gallery collapsed beneath the weakened foundations, the whole section of wall was brought down. The mine was of course powerless against a fortress built on solid rock, but in any other terrain its effect could be deadly, particularly when aimed at the angled corners of a square tower; by undermining the corner only there was a good chance of bringing down a large part of the two walls. As we shall see later, this was one of the factors that led to the change from the square tower to the round tower in the 12th century.

Once the walls were breached, the attackers would try to break into the fortifications in sufficient numbers to establish themselves inside and to prevent the defenders from repairing the damage. But the attackers might attempt to carry the wall without breaching it either by using scaling ladders or with a siege tower or belfry. The word (in French *beffroi* and in German *Berchfrit*) originally meant a place of refuge and was applied to fortified towers such as the *Berchfrit* at the Wartburg. Later it was used to describe the high, mobile tower that was wheeled up to the walls of the castle as a vantage point from which the besiegers could shoot down on the defenders. The difference in height was a considerable disadvantage for the attacking army in any siege, and the belfry provided one means of overcoming it. It had to be tall enough to overtop the walls, and strong enough and large enough to carry a considerable number of men. At the siege of Bothwell castle by Edward I in 1301, one of the belfries used was built in the neighbouring town of Glasgow, and 30 wagons were needed to transport it the nine miles to the siege operations. Such clumsy yet formidable structures were obviously made of timber, and consequently had to be covered with wet hides

to protect them from the garrison's fire arrows. When, with immense

Left, a fine example of battering on the towers of the Constable's Gate at Dover Castle. By giving a wall a batter—that is, by widening it at its base—the architect made the sappers' and miners' job more difficult or even impossible.

Below left, a superb battle scene from a mid-13th-century French manuscript showing the attackers pressing hard on the heels of a sortie as it retreats through the main gate of the castle. The engineer in charge of the trebuchet seems to be in difficulties.

Below, sappers have made a dangerous breach in the walls by tearing out the lower courses of masonry (from a 14th-century manuscript).

51

labour, they had been wheeled up to the walls, the soldiers would attempt the assault with the support of reinforcements climbing up from below, leaping down on to the battlements or even crossing over the drawbridge with which some belfries were equipped.

In the siege of a great fortress such as Château Gaillard, some or all of the devices described above were used. Both sides would have had one or more pieces of artillery with which to attack either the fortifications or the siege towers; the air would have been filled with a hail of missiles, arrows, rocks, flaming fire balls. At one point of the wall, a sapping operation might be in progress under constant attack from above. The cat protecting the sappers might eventually catch fire; the men underneath would then dash panic-stricken back to their own lines, while many of them were picked off from the walls as they ran. For the next attack, the cat might be reinforced by a belfry, which, by sweeping the walls with covering fire, would allow

The early 15th-century miniature, left, showing a French castle under siege includes an early type of siege gun. The development of gunpowder changed the whole nature of siege artillery and eventually led to the abandonment of the castle as a military strongpoint.

Below left, a mid-13th-century representation of a battering ram in action against the gate of a castle; usually the attackers would have been protected by some form of penthouse covering.

Below, a 14th-century representation of a siege tower or belfry. Here the structure has been left exposed by the artist, but in reality it would have been hung with wet hides to protect it against fire arrows.

the sappers to work relatively undisturbed. Faced with such a serious assault, the garrison might sally out from a postern gate and capture or destroy the belfry.

The sortie, besides its effect on morale, was an important part of the tactics of defence. A successful foray from the walls might manage to destroy and silence one of the enemy siege engines, or to bring back supplies from the surrounding countryside. But the most successful sortie was one that met up with a friendly force marching to the relief of the siege. The prospect of a relieving army could have an important effect on the morale of the garrison—and also on the methods of the besiegers. If no army were threatening, the besiegers might decide to starve out the defenders or to neutralise them by building a counter-castle (in German, *Gegenburg*) at the approaches. The main army could then continue the campaign without fear that its lines of communication were in danger.

Below, a 13th-century French miniature. While the attacking cavalry are engaged in a melée with knights of the garrison, soldiers try to sap the masonry and scale the walls of the fortress. In the background a trebuchet has been used for the execution of an important prisoner.

54

General developments in castle architecture

As a rough generalisation, one can say that the two centuries between 1000 and 1200 saw the full development of the medieval castle from a simple stone tower to a complex fortress with several lines of defence. Throughout this period (and slightly before and after it), the construction of any major fortification was largely dictated by the lie of the land. A castle was essentially a fortified site, so that the site itself was the prime factor in determining the kind of structures raised upon it.

As we have already pointed out, castles had been built in Europe long before the year 1000. During this period, Europe was still scattered with the remains of Roman buildings, of which some were demolished and their stones used for building churches, while others were to become strongly fortified sites. Good examples are the arena at Arles, which grew into a walled town whose houses were built on the tiers of the amphitheatre, and the Castel Sant' Angelo at Rome. Indeed, by the 11th century, the Castel Sant' Angelo (built by the Roman Emperor Hadrian as his own mausoleum) had become the

The Castel Sant' Angelo, Rome, was built on the site of an alleged miracle during the pontificate of Gregory I; the angel statue commemorates the event. Here the great drum of Roman masonry with its many later additions can be clearly seen.

55

main fortress of the popes and continued to be fortified throughout the middle ages. The cynical words of the 17th-century English philosopher Thomas Hobbes seemed to have their basis in fact when he said: 'The Papacy is not other than the Ghost of the deceased Roman Empire, sitting crowned upon the grave thereof.'

During the ninth century, the countries of Europe that were governed by the successors of the great Emperor Charlemagne were forced to defend themselves against the depredations of the Vikings. In 862, Charles the Bald (who ruled over a kingdom that was roughly equivalent to modern France) issued a decree authorising the building of castles against the invaders. But even at this early date, castles were already seen as a potential threat to the king's sovereignty, for only two years later Charles was ordering the destruction of all castles built without royal warrant. During the first three centuries of the Christian era, the *pax romana* had maintained the Empire in a state of such settled peace that the walled town, so characteristic a feature of civilisation from the earliest times, was a rare sight except on the frontiers. But during the troubled times that followed the collapse of Rome, people were forced to make their own arrangements for defence. In 867, another decree went out ordering that all the towns between the Loire and the Seine rivers should be fortified with walls. For just as the great empire of Rome eventually disintegrated, so the authority of the Carolingians declined, though much more rapidly than that of the Roman emperors. Within a century of Charlemagne's death in 814, the lands he had held, stretching from the Elbe to the frontiers of Muslim Spain and from the North Sea to central Italy, were contested by a growing number of petty, but in their own lands powerful, lords. And from their struggles developed the forces that were to shape the new political geography of Europe.

It was in this turbulent society that the castle came into its own. Originally built as a shield against the heathen pirates from beyond the borders of Christendom, it developed as the focus and symbol of the power wielded by the strong man of the neighbourhood and the base for his marauding excursions against his neighbours—excursions that might lead to the acquisition of sizeable tracts of territory. One of the most dynamic and powerful of these new families of robber barons was the house of Anjou, traditionally descended from the devil and destined to gain the crown of England as well as large holdings in France, for which they were theoretically the liegemen of the French king. Under the great Count Fulk Nerra the influence of the family spread throughout the surrounding districts. This power

The stone keep at Niort built by Henry Plantagenet in 1155. Essentially, it was an elaboration of the simple stone tower (one of the earliest types of European castle) but the rounder contours of the corner turrets mark it as a building of the transitional stage before the general adoption of round towers in the 13th century.

was consolidated with castles, of which the stone keeps of Langeais and Loches still survive. Like the towers in the Italian town of San Gimigniano and the original keep of the castle of Chillon, they represent the first principal type of medieval castle. Basically, this was a stone tower (though wood and brick were also used in districts where stone was difficult to come by), probably surrounded by a ditch and a palisade. The tower would consist of a ground-floor room, containing the castle well and ample storage space; a first-floor hall, which would include the living quarters for the lord and his followers, and perhaps a third floor with more private apartments for the lord and his family. As we have seen, the entrance to this kind of castle was usually at first-floor level, and was approached either by a wooden stairway (which could be quickly destroyed in time of siege) or by a stone stairway. If in stone, the approach stair might be protected by an outbuilding, of which a good example survives at Loches.

In England during the 10th century Alfred the Great's successor built a number of forts (or *burhs*), particularly on the frontier with

In medieval Italy, far more than in any other European country, the aristocracy resided in towns. This panorama of San Gimignano, above, shows the fortified towers built by powerful families both to defend themselves and to advertise their greatness.

Opposite, a view of the castle at Loches showing the 10th-century keep and, in the foreground, the curtain wall and towers of a later period. 59

NANT:CONTRA   DINANTES:ET:C

Wales. The exact nature of these is not clear; most may have been walled towns, but some no doubt would have been similar to the castles on the continent. But whatever their form they were royal works—a fact that reflects a crucial difference between the island kingdom, already groping towards a form of centralised royal government, and the countries of continental Europe, which was a patchwork of conflicting jurisdictions and powers. Castles in the strict sense were not properly established in England until the arrival of the Norman conquerors, whose need to defend their position in a hostile land led to the rapid spread of castles all over England. The famous Bayeux tapestry depicts the type of castle that the Normans brought with them—indeed brought with them in the most literal sense, for William included in his armaments a wooden fort that was reassembled on the shores of England. Some of the castles built by the new king and his followers—such as the Tower of London, Rochester, Canterbury and Corfe—were strong stone structures like the continental castles we have already referred to, but the vast

Two scenes from the 11th-century Bayeux tapestry. Above, a wooden motte-and-bailey castle under attack with fire and, right, a motte-and-bailey castle built in part from prefabricated sections brought over by William from Normandy.

DE RETVR : CASTELLVM : AT HESTENGA CEASTRA HIC WILL

majority were the motte-and-bailey type common in Normandy but rarely found elsewhere.

In its simplest form, this type of castle was an earth mound, either natural or artificial, surmounted by a wooden fort surrounded by a bailey and enclosed by a palisade, which would probably be defended on its outer side by a ditch. The central motte would probably be separated from the bailey by another ditch or perhaps even by a water moat running round its base. The fort would be approached over a drawbridge and up a wooden causeway set in the steeply sloping sides of the motte. This simple formula could be varied in an infinite number of ways according to the wealth of the builder, the nature of the terrain or the importance of the castle. The motte might be set on the perimeter of the palisade with the bailey projecting out in front of it; or there might be two or sometimes more baileys, separated from one another by a ditch and connected by fortified gates and drawbridges; or finally—though extremely rarely—the fort on the motte might be built of stone. Motte-and-bailey castles had an

61

obvious advantage: they could be speedily built and yet were effective enough to repel the ill-armed peasantry—important considerations for an army of conquerors. On the other hand, they were dangerously vulnerable to fire, and were much less durable than buildings made of stone. As the 12th century progressed, stone was increasingly used by castle builders. For this reason (and because most earlier timber fortifications have disappeared), we shall be dealing exclusively with the stone castles of Europe from now on.

As we shall see, many of these later stone works incorporate the mounds of earlier motte-and-bailey castles. A fine example exists at Windsor. Yet building a stone keep on an artificial motte obviously needed care. Usually, the foundations of the new stone structure were dug down into the solid earth underneath the motte, so that it became not so much a hill on which the tower was built as a defensive skirt around the base of the walls.

The keep—or, to use the French term, *donjon*—was the basic unit of European castles up to the end of the 12th century. The outer baileys and their buildings provided shelter for members of the garrison, stable space for the horses and sanctuary for the communities of the surrounding area in time of war. The keep was the last

Above, the 11th-century shell keep at Restormel in Cornwall.

Right, the 11th-century square Norman keep at Richmond.

refuge when the outer defences had fallen, and might, if shrewdly defended, hold out for many months. The actual design of the keep varied, and by the 11th century square keeps were already beginning to be replaced by shell keeps (good examples of shell keeps are to be found at Launceston and Restormel in Cornwall, and at the 12th-century castle of Gisors in Normandy). Basically, the shell keep was a hollow fortress built round a central courtyard, but its main advantage was that it was round. As we have seen, the angular corners of a square keep were particularly vulnerable to the mine—one of the most ancient and one of the most effective techniques of warfare—since the successful undermining of a single corner would bring down a considerable part of its two walls. As the 12th century progressed, the circular keep and wall tower became more and more common, although some builders attempted to work out a compromise that would combine the advantages of the square keep's regular plan with the defensive strength of the round type. Examples of such 'transitional' keeps can be found at Provins and Houdan in northern France.

Another new principle of fortification, developed in Europe and the crusading states of Syria towards the end of the 12th century, was that of the concentric fortress. (This may have first developed fully in the Hospitaller castles in the Levant, though the idea of a central stronghold defended by a number of outworks was as old as the motte-and-bailey itself, and the increasing strength of the curtain walls of the castle—an essential feature of the concentric plan—was largely dictated by the growing power of the new siege engines. On balance however, the development of the new style of fortress in the crusader states was the result both of their builders' European experience and of their study of the great Byzantine works in Syria.) Two almost text-book examples of the concentric castle are to be found in Britain: the Tower of London, which gradually acquired its outer defensive walls and towers, and the castle of Beaumaris in Anglesey, which seems to have been designed as a whole. Beaumaris is interesting not only for its symmetrical design but because it seems never to have been used. For although it was begun after one of the most dangerous Welsh rebellions, this revolt turned out to be the last. At Beaumaris the keep has disappeared; instead (as at Harlech, another concentric castle in Wales) there is a heavily fortified gatehouse. Beaumaris is defended by a moat, which originally flowed into the Menai Strait, and two curtain walls well protected by projecting round towers. The main gatehouse, on the south side of

Opposite, the shell keep at Gisors built by Henry of England in the 12th century.

the inner curtain wall, is defended by a strong outwork, or barbican, and is situated in such a way that the attacker, once he has successfully forced the outer gate, has to move across the line of fire from the inner wall to reach the next entrance. This kind of deep and elaborate defence was almost essential at Beaumaris, which is surrounded by flat land. But even in the hilly terrain of Harlech or Rhuddlan or on the craggy eminences of Château Gaillard or Krak, the concentric fortress proved to be the most advanced and effective type of defensive system. It is found in various guises all over the territories once belonging to the Emperor Charlemagne.

The span of this book is almost entirely limited to the medieval centuries, since this is the period during which the castle was not only a major element in warfare but also the focus of the life led by the European nobility. The songs of the troubadours were first heard within the walls of the castle, and the whole new social code based on the conventions of courtly love was developed there. For the peasant, the castle was often the seat of his local court and was often the harbourage of a ruthless and bloody soldiery; for the king, the castle was

Above, an aerial view of the castle at Beaumaris in Anglesey, which clearly shows the concentric shape of the plan.

Opposite, an example of a round keep at Tonquedec in Brittany.

an important factor in framing his policies, since he had to consider not only the administration of his own castles but to assess the threat to his authority posed by the castles belonging to the nobility. In this introduction, some account has been given of life in the castle, the nature of its defences and of its enemies. For the rest of the book, some of the great buildings themselves will be looked at in closer detail and their position in history and legend described. Castles continued to be built and cities fortified into the 18th century, but the new destructive power of gunpowder led to modifications such as the squat, sturdy walls of Deal in Kent. But even though castles persisted as military strongholds and the houses of the great continued to be dressed in military garb—a tendency already apparent in the 14th century at Vufflens in Switzerland and Bodiam in Kent—the castle never again occupied the same position as the focus of European secular culture.

Right, a view of Deal Castle illustrates the typical low contour of fortifications built after the development of gunpowder into a really effective weapon of war.

Below, a view of Harlech from the east showing how the low outer curtain wall of the concentric plan could be covered by the firepower of the inner curtain. The gatehouse is strongly guarded by the two large outer towers and the two smaller towers within the walls and was formerly approached across the drawbridge.

CHAPTER 1

THE TOWER OF LONDON

The two most famous English castles, the castle at Windsor and the Tower of London, have several points in common. They are both sited on the River Thames: both were used as royal residences from an early period; and both have been the scene of great events in British history. The two castles were also part of an elaborate system of fortifications built by William the Conqueror to consolidate his hold on London: Windsor was one of the fortresses controlling the approaches to London whereas the Tower was built to guard the capital itself. The existing castle lies on the Thames embankment overlooking the river just east of the 19th-century Tower Bridge, at the heart of the ever-growing sprawl of Greater London. But when it was built by William I, the White Tower stood within a few yards of the city's east wall—the wall of the old Roman town.

Unlike Windsor, the Tower has never lost the forbidding aspect of a military stronghold. Through nine centuries, successive royal builders have added to its fortifications, so that today the original tower lies at the centre of a building that is an almost classic example of the concentric castle. From earliest times, it has been used as an armoury and as the country's chief state prison for a succession of high-ranking captives; it was also the site of execution for traitors and enemies of the state. Today it is a museum of the nation's history, housing not only (among other valuables) the magnificent crown jewels of England, but also memories of such famous and tragic figures as Lady Jane Grey, Anne Boleyn, Sir Thomas More, Robert Devereux, Earl of Essex and Sir Walter Raleigh. But here our first concern must be with the castle from a military point of view, and with the various changes and additions that have produced the present fortress.

The kingdom claimed and conquered by William, Duke of Nor-

A comparison of this aerial view with the engraving on p. 79 and the sketch plan on p. 74 provides an interesting picture of the development of the Tower since the 14th century. All the buildings inside the inner ward, except the White Tower and the chapel of St Peter date from the Tudor period or later and replace earlier structures that have long since disappeared.

mandy in 1066 had the most centralised government in Europe at the time. There were of course powerful families, whose interests clashed with those of the monarchy and whose influence constantly threatened royal power. In theory, the monarchy was elective and in fact, it was by right of election that Earl Harold Godwinson claimed to be the lawful successor to the childless king Edward the Confessor. From the days of Alfred the Great, however, the house of Wessex had established itself so firmly as the ruling house that by the mid-11th century the elective principle had been discredited. And although Edward was obliged to marry the daughter of the powerful Earl Godwin, he resisted attempts to make him nominate Godwin's son Harold as his heir; instead he chose his cousin Duke William of Normandy, to whom he made the English nobility, even Earl Harold himself, swear an oath of allegiance. The authority of the Anglo-Saxon kings throughout the country, modelled on that of the papal curia, was far greater than that of the Capetian kings of France. The chance to exercise this power was acquired by Duke William after his defeat of Harold—a chance that he seized with both hands. Yet in spite of his genuine claim to the throne, the years following his victory at Hastings were marked by unrest and rebellion, and control of London—the capital of the increasingly centralised monarchy—became the cornerstone of William's authority. For this reason, elaborate precautions were taken to defend it, and the massive keep—known to later generations as the White Tower— began to be built on the east boundary of London.

The first structure, possibly a motte-and-bailey castle, was sited so that the old Roman wall (repaired by King Alfred some three centuries earlier) provided a bulwark to the east. But in the late 1070s Gundulf of Bec—soon to be Bishop of Rochester, the site of another great stone keep—was put in charge of the building of the massive stone tower we see today. Its external appearance has changed very little since it was built nine centuries ago, although many of the larger windows were given a neo-classical form by Sir Christopher Wren and the setting has of course been completely altered by the surrounding buildings and courtyard. A more basic change is the disappearance of the original entrance. This was on the south side and, like the entrance at Rochester and many other towers of the period, was at first-floor level approached by an external stairway.

The White Tower is 90 feet high and its ground plan is roughly square. Its shape is in fact made irregular by the apse of the Chapel of St John, which is accommodated by a projection in the walls at the

This miniature from a manuscript of the poems of Charles d'Orléans (c. 1500) depicts the duke leaning out of a window of the White Tower where he was imprisoned for several years after his capture at the Battle of Agincourt (1415). In the background can be seen the shops and houses on the old London Bridge.

All but three items of the Crown Jewels were sold during the Commonwealth (1649–60), the brief period in which the English lived without a king. Above left, the anointing spoon (late 12th century) and the eagle ampulla (14th century), which are used for the anointing of the sovereign during the coronation service. The orb, crown and sceptres, above, are all post-Restoration in date.

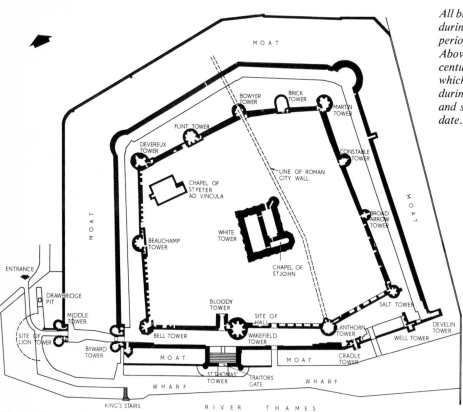

The sketch plan of the medieval Tower of London, left, reveals a concentric castle of almost copybook perfection. As explained, this was the result of developments stretching over the centuries.

Left, the White Tower, the central stronghold of the Tower of London. It was built by William the Conqueror and has changed little since his day; the main difference is the windows, which were given their present neo-classical aspect by Sir Christopher Wren. The Tower, like many castles in the middle ages, was originally whitewashed—and so gained its name. The projection from the eastern corner, seen here, contains the chapel of St John.

Below, St John's Chapel, a superb example of Norman architecture (c. 1080) that survives virtually unaltered. It occupies the upper two floors, so that major alterations have been impossible, and has only two outside walls, so the fabric has been protected against the weather.

south-east corner, and a projecting round turret strengthening the north-east corner. The other three corners are protected by square turrets rising above the level of the battlements. Internally the tower is divided down the centre by a wall running the length of its north-south axis. (Again, there is a similar wall at Rochester, although there it is breached at third-floor level by a large hall extending across both halves of the building.) The Tower is roughly 110 feet square—an area large enough to contain two spacious and stately halls in the west half alone; these are the Council Room (now called the Horse Armoury) on the top floor and the Banqueting Room (the Weapon Room) on the first floor. Apart from these two magnificent halls, the keep contains five other smaller chambers, all of which are used today to house the Tower's collection of armour and weapons. But without doubt, the finest part of the White Tower, of the whole fortress, and indeed perhaps of any castle in Europe, is the Chapel of St John, which occupies the two upper floors of the south-east part of the keep.

The chapel is as rich in historical associations as anywhere else in the fortress: here, for example, Queen Mary was betrothed by proxy to Philip II of Spain. As the inner chapel of a great fortress that was in constant occupation throughout its long history, it is remarkably well preserved. It therefore provides us with a superb example of a type of building that all too often has been destroyed or allowed to fall into ruin. Above all, this little Norman chapel with its superimposed arcades of rounded arches, the simplicity of its vaulting and its atmosphere of intimate devotion is a place of overwhelming beauty and pathos. It mirrors in miniature the massive architecture of the great cathedral at Durham, and both buildings, each noble in its own way, express the determination of the conquerors to dominate the land that they had seized with the blessing of Holy Mother Church.

For a century, the Tower begun by William the Conqueror and completed under his son William Rufus stood on guard over the capital. As might be expected, it played an important part in the civil wars between Stephen and Matilda, and once again became the key point of royal control over the city of London during the reign of the next king, Henry II. One of Henry's first moves was to weaken or destroy the illegitimate castles belonging to the barons and to strengthen those in royal hands. With this aim in mind, he fortified the motte of the castle at Windsor with a stone tower in place of the wooden one built by the Conqueror. But the great stone walls of the Tower of London did not seem to need reinforcing, and it was not

76

Above, the Middle Tower (to the right) and the Byward Tower; in the background part of Tower Bridge can be seen across the river. These two gates formed the second and third entrances respectively of the medieval castle. The main outer entrance was formerly the Lion Gate and the Lion Tower, now disappeared (see the sketch plan on p. 74).

Opposite, the Bell Tower designed for Richard I but built in the first years of the 13th century; Sir Thomas More was among those imprisoned here. Behind it can be seen the former Lieutenant's Lodgings, built in the reign of Henry VIII and renamed the Queen's House in the 1880s.

until he was succeeded by his son Richard I, the most notable military architect of his age, that any improvements or additions were made to the fortress at the capital. All that remains of the building work begun during Richard's reign (in other words, during the 1190s), and completed during the first years of the 13th century, is the Bell Tower in the south-west corner of the inner wall and a stretch of the south curtain. The rest of the inner enceinte and its various towers date from many different periods of building and reconstruction. Except for the Wakefield and Bloody Towers, the south wall beyond the stretch of 12th-century work is a 19th-century reconstruction, which, as had been revealed by recent excavation, is slightly off the line of the original walls; the east and north walls and their towers almost all date from the troubled reign of Henry III, while the west wall was built in the time of his son, Edward I.

As a result of King Richard's work, continued and rebuilt by his successors, the Tower of London was transformed into a concentric castle of simple form—a type of fortification that became increasingly popular as the 13th century progressed. At the end of the century, additional work commissioned by Edward I, architect of the great Welsh castles, completed the metamorphosis of the simple, if mighty, keep of the first Norman king into a sophisticated, even fashionable fortress. After Edward's reign, a number of comparatively minor additions were made under Edward III, Richard II and Henry VIII, of which the most important is the 14th-century chapel of St Peter ad Vincula. From the 17th century onwards, various other structures were added during successive building periods. These include the New Armouries and the Waterloo Barracks, which now line the inner circuit of the original curtain wall.

Even today, the Tower of London looks extremely formidable; in its heyday it was very strong indeed. Recent excavations seem to show that the Bell Tower, Wakefield Tower and indeed the whole of the south curtain wall of the inner enceinte were washed by the Thames; at this period, of course, the other walls were protected by a moat. But from the time of Edward I, the south side was doubly defended both by the river (which could of course also be used for sending men and supplies to relieve the garrison by water) and by the moat, which encircled all four walls and divided the castle wall from the wharf. On the north and west, the moat is over 100 feet wide, while at the south-west corner it was diverted to give extra protection to an elaborate system of entrance bridges and gates. Any attacking force attempting to enter the castle through the main gate of the

Byward Tower first had to defile over a narrow bridge, parallel to the western wall and passing over a channel. (This channel branched out from the main moat to form a semicircular bend around the fortifications of the middle tower.) The bridge was defended on the land side by a gate and its central portion consisted of a drawbridge. The next stage in the defences of this complicated entrance, the large semicircular Lion Tower, has completely disappeared, but stones have been set in the roadway to show the line of its walls. Once inside the tower, the attackers had to take a right-angled turn to cross a second drawbridge protected by the Middle Gate; this led to a third and final drawbridge across the main moat to the Byward Tower.

The Tower of London has been continuously occupied throughout its history. It has kept its military associations up to the present day, and is still garrisoned. As appropriate to its role as the greatest fortress in the land, it was involved—if by chance—in the Second World War, when it received its last bombardment by German aeroplanes. Its fortifications were strengthened for the last time as late 78 as 1846 (the year in which the Duke of Wellington himself was called upon to mobilise the defence of London against the Chartists), when an additional bastion was built on to the north part of the outer enceinte. Its history as a state prison ended even more recently, during the present century: the last prisoner to be held within its walls was Hitler's deputy, Rudolf Hess. One result of the Tower's continuous use is its fine state of preservation. The modern visitor can still sense some of the despair felt by the unfortunate prisoners who passed through the Traitor's Gate, the river entrance beneath the St Thomas Tower, and feel the hopelessness of their confinement in the many wall towers such as the notorious Bloody Tower.

Today the Tower of London has a double value: both for the richness of its historical associations and for the golden opportunity it offers for studying the techniques of medieval fortification. The magnificent collection of arms and armour housed in the White Tower—the legacy of the enthusiasm of a royal collector, Henry VIII —gives a clear idea of the weapons with which the great fortresses were defended and attacked, and helps us to understand more fully the fear and respect that they inspired in their time.

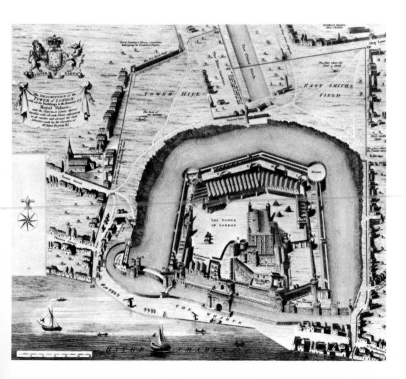

A view of the Tower of London based on a survey of 1597. It shows clearly how, on the river side, the fortress was defended not only by the Thames itself but also by the moat running inside the wharf. A particularly interesting feature is the extension to the moat around the former Lion's Tower and the Middle Tower forming an almost insurmountable series of obstacles to the main entrance of the fortress itself.

CHAPTER 2

WINDSOR

The castle of Windsor, the chief residence of the English royal house and the largest inhabited castle in the world, stands on a low hill on the south bank of the River Thames overlooking the little modern town of Windsor. To the south, stretches Windsor Great Park, reached from the castle by the Long Walk; to the east, Home Park runs down to the river. The calm and elegant beauty of the setting and the marked residential character of the castle itself tend to obscure the natural strength of the site, so that, in spite of the mighty curtain wall and its towers, the visitor may be tempted to forget the castle's original purpose and to think only of the chivalry, pomp and elegance of its later history.

The metamorphosis from fortress to residence is common enough, but at Windsor this process is particularly interesting. Many of the castles studied in this book have been restored, sometimes extensively at various times, but almost always the restorers aimed—on the whole successfully—to recover the authentic appearance of the original. At Windsor, the buildings put up by successive sovereigns have radically changed the castle's character; in particular, the considerable programme of rebuilding carried out during the reign of George IV was aimed at providing a residence that was comfortable and elegant by contemporary standards. At this time, fashionable taste was beginning to acquire a Gothic flavour, so at Windsor we have a fascinating juxtaposition of the fragments of a genuine medieval fortress and an early 19th-century conception of a medieval fortress. In this chapter, therefore, we shall be concentrating mainly on the castle built by the Norman kings and by the later Plantagenets with a brief look, by way of comparison, at the work of

Sir Jeffry Wyatville during the early 19th century. We shall largely

Above, a panoramic view of Windsor Castle taken from the north. The skyline presented by the palace-fortress today is the result of new building under Charles II and George IV.

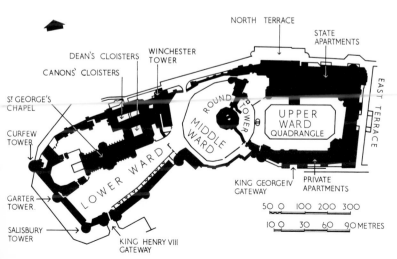

NORTH TERRACE

STATE APARTMENTS

DEAN'S CLOISTERS

WINCHESTER TOWER

CANONS' CLOISTERS

St GEORGE'S CHAPEL

ROUND TOWER

MIDDLE WARD

UPPER WARD QUADRANGLE

EAST TERRACE

CURFEW TOWER

LOWER WARD

GARTER TOWER

KING GEORGE IV GATEWAY

PRIVATE APARTMENTS

SALISBURY TOWER

KING HENRY VIII GATEWAY

50 0   100 200 300

10 0   30   60   90 METRES

Left, a sketch plan of the castle showing both the line of the medieval fortifications and the state and private apartments of Restoration and Georgian times.

81

ignore the royal apartments as such and the work of the architect Hugh May for Charles II, although these are of course an important part of the modern castle. Our principal aim is to expose as far as possible the outlines of medieval Windsor, which, with the Tower of London, was the main stronghold of the English kings in southern England during the early middle ages.

The first castle on the site was built by William the Conqueror, probably about 1070, and belonged to the early years of his vigorous consolidation of the victory at Hastings. Although many modern historians tend to regard William's right to the English throne as genuine, it was a claim that was seized by force and that had to be held by force. The castles of the invaders therefore sprang up in every English shire. With others, Windsor was built to defend the approaches to the capital, itself dominated by the great stone fortress of the White Tower. The site was not only naturally strong, protected to the north by the river and by the sharp slope of its hill, but it was also strategically well placed, since it was only a day's march from London. The first castle was a motte-and-bailey—a type described in the introduction. The motte was protected by three wards, divided from one another by a ditch and a rampart, and crowned by a wooden tower typical of many others built during the early years of the Norman occupation of England. And it is an interesting fact that this sophisticated fortress-palace, the product of centuries of development, still centres on the primitive mound of the original castle.

The next important development at Windsor took place about a century later during the reign of King Henry II. His accession in 1254 followed a period of semi-anarchy caused by the struggle for the crown between his mother Matilda, daughter of King Henry I, and King Stephen, Henry's nephew. The young Henry II Plantagenet brought with him not only vast lands in France—some inherited from his father Geoffrey, Count of Anjou, and others acquired by his marriage to Eleanor of Aquitaine—but also an active determination to restore order in his new kingdom. Henry's most pressing problem was to arrest the decline of the strong, centralised state of the first three Norman kings into a patchwork of feuding seigniories. The danger was highlighted by the number of unauthorised or 'adulterine' castles that had sprung up during the confused reign of Stephen. One of the new king's first tasks was to destroy these petty strongholds—a task that he carried through with vigour and thoroughness. A natural corollary of this policy was to strengthen the seats of royal power, so it is not surprising that during Henry's reign the wooden fortifications

82

Right, the East Terrace where, at the point furthest from the massive south-west curtain wall of Henry III, the castle has abandoned all pretensions to military status. The stately private apartments of the sovereign, built by Sir Jeffry Wyatville for George IV, overlooking cool lawns and ornamental gardens are far removed from the stern necessities of defence.

In this view of the Round Tower (above right) the slope of the original Norman motte on which it stands can be clearly seen; the upper two floors and the machicolations are part of the 19th-century reconstruction of the castle by Wyatville.

Far right, part of the south-west curtain wall, the Garter Tower and Curfew Tower, dating from the reign of Henry III. The tiled roof of the Curfew Tower (furthest from the camera) was added during the 19th-century restorations, but during the middle ages all the towers would probably have been roofed in this way.

at Windsor were replaced by a stone tower and stone walls. Of these only the lower masonry courses of the great Round Tower on the original Norman motte, survive; the apartments built for Henry in the Upper and Lower wards have long since disappeared.

As one of the greatest rulers in English history, Henry not only re-established royal authority after a period of great weakness but laid the foundations of a new legal system, which brought all Englishmen within the jurisdiction of a common law that overrode local custom or baronial privilege. But the achievements of his reign bore bitter fruit for the sons who succeeded him. The Angevin Empire in France was eroded in spite of the military genius of Richard the Lionheart and in spite of his great fortress at Château Gaillard, while in England the barons' resentment against royal restraint on their privileges finally brought King John to Runnymede. During these years, the castle at Windsor withstood the only two sieges of its long

Above, a view from the Long Walk of the King George IV Gateway and the South Terrace by Wyatville illustrating the way in which the 19th-century rebuilding combined the requirement for spacious and elegant living accommodation with the decorative use of medieval motifs. To the left of the gateway can be seen the medieval Edward III Tower.

Left, a shot taken from inside the Middle Ward showing the so-called Norman Gateway—in fact, part of the works undertaken during the reign of Edward III.

history, first in 1193, when the castle was taken and garrisoned by Prince John during his brother's absence on the Third Crusade, and again in 1215 when John himself was besieged—unsuccessfully—by the rebellious barons. Magna Carta, the great charter of baronial liberties, became a source of friction between John's son and successor Henry III and his nobles: like his father, he was faced with civil war and rebellion. So it is hardly surprising that the next stage of the fortifications at Windsor was completed under him; the three sturdy towers of the south-west wall, the Salisbury, Garter and Curfew Towers, are the main structures surviving from his reign. Of these, the Curfew Tower was given its present conical roof during the 1860s. Possibly all three were originally covered in this way.

The next great period of building at Windsor took place during the reign of Edward III, when the castle was enriched with a new series of royal apartments and became the centre of the new Order of the Garter, the first of the European orders of chivalry. The works at Windsor during the 1350s were supervised by William Wykeham, whose appointment as surveyor of the king's works in 1356 marked the real launching of a brilliant career that led him from his serf origins to the bishopric of Winchester and a high position among the king's advisers. During his time at Windsor, Wykeham began his association with the mason William of Wynford—an association that produced the royal lodgings of Edward III at Windsor, the buildings for Wykeham's foundations at Winchester College and New College, Oxford, and the new nave at Winchester Cathedral.

The Lower Ward at Windsor with St George's Chapel on the left and the Norman Gateway and the Round Tower in the background. This view gives a good idea of the largeness of the area enclosed by the circuit of the curtain walls in a major medieval fortress.

Although little remains of the works built for Edward III (except the so-called Norman Gateway to the north of the Round Tower, which still survives), an inscription on the Winchester Tower, built under Henry III but largely reconstructed under William of Wykeham, provides a vivid reminder of this great period in the castle's history and its importance in the career of one of the most important figures in history of 14th-century English architecture. The inscription reads *Hoc fecit Wykeham Anno Domini 1356*, which is said to have angered King Edward, who took the Latin words to mean 'This made Wykeham'; his young clerk of the works hastened to assure him that all that was intended was the simple statement of fact, 'Wykeham made this'. Both statements, as it turned out, were true. And as we shall see, some 500 years later the Winchester Tower provided the lodging for another architect who might claim that Windsor had made him.

During the late 17th century, King Charles II made many alterations to the castle and most of the present state apartments are contained in the house built for him and his queen, Catherine of Braganza, by the architect Hugh May. But, as has already been explained, the only post-medieval addition to claim our attention here is the major 'improvement' carried through for King George IV. The contract was won by Jeffry Wyatt in competition with the famous John Nash, builder of the Pavilion at Brighton, the new houses in Regent Street and the terraces of Regent's Park, London, and Robert Smirke, architect of the neo-classical façade of the British Museum. It is easy to see how the romantic medievalism of Wyatt's design must have seemed more appropriate at a time when the diversity of styles during the Regency period was about to give way to a hardening preference for neo-Gothic. Wyatt, who was given rooms in the Winchester Tower, was responsible for building the East Terrace, the royal apartments to the east and south of the Upper Ward quadrangle, the George IV Gate and for the present appearance of the Round Tower. Wyatt's aim was to produce an elegant, well-proportioned residence for his royal patron, and the squat, stone medieval structure did not provide a sufficiently dominating centrepiece for his grand composition. He therefore raised the walls of the Round Tower by about 30 feet, and fitted it with a series of machicolations, battlements and a turret. The expense of these works and the other improvements to the interiors made under Wyatt's direction was met by a parliamentary grant of £715,000; they took four years to complete, earned Wyatt a knighthood and royal permission to change his name to Wyatville.

From a moderately successful architect he became fashionable and

In the aerial view, opposite, the origins of the castle at Windsor as a simple motte-and-bailey fort, built by William I, are obvious; the Round Tower and its hill are the hub of the castle.

Below, the west end of St George's Chapel. The window represents the final flowering of the Perpendicular style; it was completed in 1509 and its glass depicts popes, kings, saints and princes.

The main entrance to Windsor, the King Henry VIII Gateway, with the arms of Henry and the pomegranate emblem of his first queen, Catherine of Aragon, carved above it. Despite its towers, provisions for a portcullis and the machicolations, the structure, like so much of the surviving building at Windsor, reflects the residential character acquired by the castle.

sought-after; whatever others may have thought, he seems to have considered his work at Windsor to have been his greatest achievement, for he emblazoned his George IV Gate on his coat of arms.

Admittedly Wyatville achieved his aim of building a splendid and palatial residence for the monarch, but we shall have a truer picture of the castle as a castle if we try and picture it during the reign of Henry III. At this time, the curtain wall followed its present line, but was defended all along its circuit with towers, which, like those on the south-west wall, would have stood out as the castle's main features; the three wards, the Lower, Middle and Upper, were probably divided from one another by walls guarded by a ditch and towers and through which one passed by a gateway protected by a drawbridge. The inhabitants would have been accommodated inside low buildings, probably built of wattle and timber, and the whole fortress would have been dominated by the squat, sturdy Round Tower built by Henry II. The chief addition made to the buildings inside the walls during the 13th century was the Chapel of St Edward the Confessor (dedicated in 1249), which survived in its original state until 1863, when it was restored by order of Queen Victoria. It had, however, ceased to be the main chapel of the castle much earlier, when the Chapel of St George was completed in the early 16th century. It is to this building—one of the finest examples of the English Perpendicular style and one of the most important of the buildings at Windsor—that we must now turn our attention.

The Chapel of St George was begun in 1477 on the orders of Edward IV, continued by his successors, Richard III, Henry VII and Henry VIII, and completed in 1528. Its great glory is the superb fanvaulting which, with that at Bath Abbey and King's College Chapel, Cambridge, represents one of the finest examples of this characteristic feature of the late Perpendicular style. (Incidentally, it is interesting to note that the masons in charge of the work were associated with the buildings at Bath and Cambridge.) But the fame of St George's Chapel at Windsor rests less on its artistic merits than on its status as the Chapel of the Order of the Garter. Over the magnificently carved choir stalls, the work of William Berkeley, hang the banners of the knights of the order and over the stalls are their arms displayed on enamelled shields. The order was founded by Edward III in the 1340s, and was given the Chapel of St Edward the Confessor as its first chapel. Its foundation might be taken as a sign of Windsor's change in function from a genuine military fortification to something approaching a royal palace. The nostalgic romanticism of the age of chivalry of the late middle ages had its roots in the reality of warfare and knighthood of an earlier period. These ideas were embodied in the Arthurian romance cycles so popular from the 12th century. In England, the best known of these is the *Morte d'Arthur*, an idyllic hymn of the chivalric virtues written by Sir Thomas Malory when a captive during the cynical and bloody conflict of the Wars of the Roses. During the same period, the knights of the Order of the Golden Fleece, founded by Duke Philip the Good of Burgundy, delighted in rich charades of pomp and ceremony similar to those of the Garter knights. It is difficult for us to assess how far (if at all) the idealistic codes of knightly behaviour revered by these European orders of chivalry influenced the often brutal and ruthless military and political careers of their members; and it would be fascinating to know to what extent the knights themselves recognised the contradictions between the ideals of their order and the realities of their lives.

It has been suggested that, by founding the Order of the Garter, Edward III brilliantly adapted the game of chivalry to his own political ends. It has been pointed out that the code of knightly honour was an effective instrument for blunting the edge of aristocratic ambition, and that while the most powerful lords of England were bound by the mystical oath of knighthood to their sovereign, the threat of rebellion and subversion would be lessened. But whatever the motives behind it, the Order of the Garter fired the imagination of Europe, inspired numerous imitations and established itself firmly in English tradition. With the foundation of the order, the development of Windsor was over; the transformation from warlike castle to palace was achieved—a transition that was symbolised by the first parade of Garter knights before the young King Edward in the castle precincts.

CHAPTER 3

KRAK DES CHEVALIERS

Krak des Chevaliers stands in the Syrian desert on a spur of black basalt rock between two converging wadis, or dried-up watercourses. On three sides the site is naturally defended by the lie of the land, which falls away sharply to the east, and rather less precipitously to the north and west. Strategically Krak was of great value as one of the castles controlling the Homs gap, the natural pass through the mountains between the main Syrian desert to the coast; it was also the main bastion guarding the road between the Muslim city of Homs and the Christian city of Tripoli. Until its fall in 1271, Krak was one of the most important crusader castles; certainly it is the most

Opposite, the chapel of Krak des Chevaliers. Particular points to notice are the blind arches down the side walls of the chapel and the Muslim pulpit to the right, installed after the capture of Krak when the chapel became a mosque.

Below, the mighty fortress of Krak des Chevaliers, the most important and impressive crusader castle in the Levant. This view shows the great talus or glacis of sloping masonry along the west and south walls and, to the east of the aqueduct, the square Islamic tower.

impressive both for its remarkable state of preservation and for the astonishing strength and complexity of its defences.

There was already a castle on the site of Krak when the first crusaders arrived in the 1090s. This castle, which was held by a Kurdish garrison—and for this reason was often referred to by Arab writers as the castle of the Kurds—passed into the hands of the Christian counts of Tripoli. But in 1142, Count Raymond II, who found the upkeep of the fortress too great a drain on his resources, sold the castle and its rich lands to the east to the Knights of the Hospital of St John of Jerusalem. And it was the Hospitallers who, over the next century, gave the castle its present shape.

The First Crusade reached its triumphant conclusion with the capture of Jerusalem in 1099 and the election of Godfrey of Bouillon as King of Jerusalem with the title of Defender of the Holy Sepulchre. During the following two centuries, the kingdom of Jerusalem and the other Latin states in the Levant were governed by feudal rulers whose political interests did not always coincide with the original purpose of the crusades. This was, in theory at least, to defend the holy places and to protect the pilgrim routes—a dual role that was increasingly assumed by the military religious orders of the Knights Templar and the Knights Hospitaller. The Hospitallers, the senior of the two orders, was founded in the 11th century to nurse sick pilgrims at the Hospital of St John in Jerusalem. It was still a nursing order when it was taken under papal protection in 1113, but from 1120 to 1160, during the grand mastership of Raymond du Puy, the Hospitallers became increasingly military in character,

Above, the castle from the east, dominating the Arab village at the foot of the hill. From this side, the approach is steep and rugged, and once dangerous too for an attacker.

Opposite, the interior of the 'ramp', leading from the main entrance on the eastern outer wall to the gate of the inner enceinte. The attacking troops, once they had broken down the outer gate, had either to face the hostile fire from the inner wall or brave this sloping vaulted passage with its 'murder' holes in the roof and unexpected sortie points for the defenders.

devoting themselves not only to the care of pilgrims on their arrival but also to their protection on their journey. With the Templars (founded in 1118), the Hospitallers represented a new element in the feudal structure of the Kingdom of Jerusalem—a military body answerable to the Church rather than to the king. Members of both orders took vows of poverty, chastity and obedience, and were pledged to draw their swords only in defence of the Cross against the Infidel. Yet though the knights themselves were poor, the corporate wealth of their orders grew enormously as pious patrons in Europe endowed them with valuable property. So as the power and resources of the secular rulers diminished during the 12th century, wealth and influence were accumulated by the orders, which gradually won control of the key points of the kingdom. From their headquarters in Jerusalem, and later from the castle of Margat, the Hospitallers administered vast tracts of land throughout the Levant.

The fortress at Krak is an outstanding example of the concentric plan, which played a vitally important part in the development of military architecture. This form of castle was particularly favoured by the Hospitallers. Even so, we must not assume that Krak was originally designed as a concentric castle in the way that Château Gaillard, for example, was. The building of Krak, which was spread over nearly 150 years, was concentrated into two main periods: during the 1140s, immediately after the Hospitallers' take-over, and during the early 1200s, after an earthquake in 1202 had made major rebuilding and redesign necessary. During this second building phase, the 12th-century castle became, with the severe modifications that will be described later, the inner enceinte of the new one. In this second castle, the line of the inner wall, built according to the lie of the land around the top of the spur, followed the wall of the earlier structure; in fact, much of the original wall remains, concealed in the later masonry. The main entrance was by way of a gate in the east wall, approached by a zig-zag path up the steep escarpment on the east side. (So attackers attempting to breach the entrance either had to scramble up the steep and rocky slope or had to follow the winding path in column, crossing and recrossing the concentrated fire from the walls of the fortress.) The main work undertaken after 1202 was the massive additional defences to the west and south walls of the first enceinte, and the construction of a second outer enceinte, which, to the west, north and south, was built immediately below the existing walls. To the east, however, it ran down the steep escarpment to include part of the approach path, and was fortified to form the

notorious ramp at Krak. Let us now take a more detailed look at these fortifications.

Obviously, the weakest part of the castle's defences was the wall to the south, where the gently sloping land broadened into the surrounding terrain. Consequently, a new line of masonry was built along the inner western and southern walls, and the earlier square towers were encased in rounded bastions, which deflected the weapons of the attacking forces more effectively and made mining more difficult. (Added protection was provided by the smooth finish of the stones, on which the besiegers were unable to attach their grappling irons.) In fact, mining these particular walls was made almost impossible by the massive *talus*, or masonry bulwark, which sloped outward from the walls and plunged some thirty feet down to the ditch between the enceintes. This *talus* extended along to the western and southern walls, while to the south was erected, as an additional precaution, the mightiest defence work in the whole repertoire of medieval fortifications. Here the ditch was excavated still deeper, and lined with stone to form a large *berquil*, or reservoir, which, besides supplying the garrison with water, confronted the attackers with a deep water-filled moat. The stone retaining wall of this moat rose steeply to join the inside of the outer enceinte and as shown on the plan, the whole complex was dominated by the three fortified towers. From the air, the full scope of the works can be seen at a glance, but from the ground, the obstacles are concealed by the wall of the outer defences. This element of surprise constitutes the

Far left, the great southern redoubt at Krak showing the Constable's Tower (on the corner of the enceinte) and the glacis sloping into the berquil *or reservoir. The full height of the glacis could only be seen after the outer walls had been reached; it is thought that it was the sight of this apparently impregnable obstacle that prompted Baybars to resort to trickery.*

Left, one of the great cellars at Krak. Here supplies would be stored and the soldiers of the garrison might also be quartered. Ventilation and light are provided by the holes in the roof.

Below, a French model of Krak, which enables us to study the layout more closely than even the best aerial photograph. This view represents the castle from the north-east. The inner curtain wall (the earlier 12th-century castle) contains the chapel with its 'chevet' projection from the wall and, round the corner, the north postern gate (extreme right). The outer wall contains the main entrance (centre) from which the ramp leads us to the left.

final subtlety of the design, for even when the outer wall had been taken, the castle was still almost impregnable. In this way, the designers of Krak overcame the weakness of the site on the southern side and transformed it into the most formidable part of the building.

To the east, the problem was different. As has already been pointed out, the lie of the land made this side of the site easy to defend; for this reason, it was here that the main entrance to the castle was situated. But because it is a major gap in the curtain wall, the main gate of any castle is always a weak spot. The designers therefore tried to divert the attackers' attention from the vulnerable entrance to the more easily defended sections of the walls. As might be expected, this aim was achieved at Krak in a particularly ingenious way. Judged by the rest of the building, the gate in the outer wall was not particularly formidable, but once it was breached, the attacker had to run the gauntlet of the first group of machicolations in the outer gate. He was then presented with a formidable choice: either he had to break out into the bailey between the two walls of defence and so expose himself to murderous crossfire or continue southward along the covered passage he had already entered. The vaulted passage, known as the great ramp, which followed the line of the zig-zag path referred to earlier, was defended by a series of machicolations, loopholes for archers, portcullises and concealed postern gates from which the defenders could spring out and take the terrified attackers unawares. And as well as all the other hazards, there was a hairpin bend to be negotiated. Following this dreadful route must have been a demoralising experience, and at the end of it, there was still the main gate of the castle to be taken.

Although the southern defences and the great ramp were undoubtedly the most heavily fortified points of the castle, all the defences were built with an equal degree of ingenuity and strength; in short, as far as humanly possible, Krak was proof against capture by storm. To have starved the garrison out would have been equally difficult. Like all great crusader castles, Krak was provided with vast storage space both for food and for water. We have already mentioned the great *berquil*—a word derived from *birke*, an Arabic word for a reservoir. Such reservoirs are found in other castles in Syria, an arid country where open and lined storage tanks were commonly used for storing rainfall. At Krak, the *berquil* (which in other fortresses was sometimes outside the fortifications), may well have been used as a welcome bathing pool for both men and horses; there were in addition as many as nine cisterns for drinking water. Inside the walls of

96

Above, the west side of the courtyard with the arcade outside the great hall. In the section in shadow on the left of the picture, the pointed arches and rosette are still intact and give some idea of original elegance of this arcade.

Right, a sketch plan of Krak. Like the Tower of London, the concentric scheme results from successive stages in the building.

Below, the Constable's Tower at the south-west corner of the inner enceinte at Krak. On the extreme right can just be seen the entrance to the tower at first-floor level; the picture also gives some idea of the commanding view from the handsome windows of the great chamber.

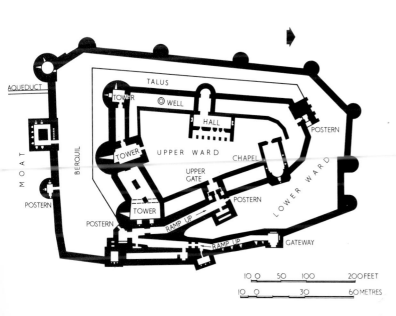

AQUEDUCT

TALUS

WELL

TOWER

HALL

POSTERN

MOAT

BEROUIL

TOWER

UPPER WARD

CHAPEL

UPPER GATE

LOWER WARD

POSTERN

POSTERN

TOWER

POSTERN

RAMP UP

RAMP UP

GATEWAY

10 0   50   100   200 FEET

10 0   30   60 METRES

the castle, massive vaulted undercrofts were used for storing grain and other foodstuffs. Perhaps the most impressive is the undercroft that runs from the north wall of the chapel around the inner perimeter of the inner enceinte—a distance of about 400 feet; almost equally imposing is the vaulted hall supporting the esplanade in the centre of the courtyard.

It has been estimated that, at full strength, the garrison of Krak would have consisted of about 2000 men. Whether Krak, or indeed any of the great crusader fortresses, ever contained its full complement is somewhat doubtful; certainly during its last years it was heavily undermanned. Even so, the wall towers, and possibly the undercrofts, could easily have accommodated the men-at-arms and mercenaries who made up the bulk of the defenders, while the knights themselves were most probably housed in the three great towers to the south. Of these, the south-west tower was almost certainly the castellan's residence; here the grand master of the order would have stayed during his visits to the castle. The tower's main chamber, entered from the wall-walk, is a handsome vaulted room with sculptured capitals and corbels and a large window decorated with floral carving. The rooms in the other two towers are pleasant but less stately than the main apartments. It was once thought that the three towers were intended to be the castle's final line of defence by forming a kind of keep. But the English scholar Cathcart King has convincingly shown that the complex would not have presented a large attacking force with any very serious problems. While admitting that the arrangement of the staircases and the access to the various rooms—particularly to the main apartments in the south-west tower—suggest some form of defensive measures, King advances an interesting theory to account for them. He suggests that the precautions taken, although inadequate to repel a hostile army, would have deterred an attempted mutiny by the mercenary garrison against the knights and the castellan.

In peacetime the chapel was the centre of life at Krak, and, as might be expected in a castle inhabited by a religious order, it is a large and elaborate building. It was constructed during the 1170s, after an earthquake had destroyed the earlier structure. Built in the Romanesque style, it measures about 65 feet by 25; at the east end the chevet projects a few feet through the curtain wall to form a defensive tower. A century later, the knights built an impressive banqueting hall by the north wall of the inner enceinte. Along the outside of the hall is a cloister gallery, notable for the elegant carving

Above, the interior of the great hall at Krak, built in the first half of the 13th century. The hall is on the west side of the courtyard and, with its soaring vaults and carved corbels, provided a dignified setting for the assemblies of the Knights Hospitaller.

The corbels at Krak, as this detail (opposite) from the cloistered arcade shows, are carved with typical motifs of the period, recalling the leafy foliage of a European landscape rather than the arid desert setting of the fortress.

of its window mullions, capitals and corbels. To help maintain the garrison, the castle was also provided with a windmill on its walls and an aqueduct running into the *berquil* through the south wall.

As well as being a castle built to withstand siege, Krak was the residence of knights belonging to one of Christendom's most powerful orders, whose pennant flew proudly from the castellan's turret. It was therefore provided with living quarters suitable for men of rank. It was a centre of the strange life led by Christians in Outremer, the land beyond the sea—an existence of continual compromise with the infidel. Thus the king of Jerusalem held audience cross-legged in the Arab manner; proud scions of great Frankish families dressed in soft, flowing Oriental garments and counted Arab scholars among their friends and courtiers; and Christian knights became learned in the scriptures of Islam. In the courts of Outremer, a witness might swear on the Koran, and the accused could be convicted only on the testimony of a co-religionist. Not surprisingly, the knights of the religious orders were less inclined to fraternise with the civilisation that they were pledged to fight; but they too, in times of peace, were obliged to come to terms with the infidel subjects who surrounded their strongholds and cultivated their land. It has been calculated that the total number of Western knights in Outremer never exceeded 3000; a policy of live and let-live was therefore inevitable.

But peaceful co-existence is no substitute for military strength. During the 13th century, as the powers of Europe turned more and more to their own affairs, the Latin states of Outremer became increasingly exposed to attack by their Muslim opponents once a leader had arisen to unite them. This leadership was provided by the Sultan Baybars (the name means a panther), a Mongol by birth who was sold into slavery first as a youth in Damascus and later to the Egyptian Mameluke Sultan Kotouz. He rose rapidly in the service of Kotouz and in 1260 assassinated his master, proclaiming himself sultan. To his political ruthlessness and military skill, Baybars added a fanatical hatred of Christianity. The Latin states were powerless to check his growing power, and after the failure in 1270 of the Eighth Crusade, no further reinforcements arrived from the West.

In March the following year the conquering Baybars stood before the forbidding walls of Krak, which during its long history had withstood twelve sieges and from whose gates even the great Saladin had turned away. But the sultan was determined on capture, and the garrison, although well able to hold out for a year or more, must have realised that there was little or no chance of relief.

There are three Arab descriptions of the siege; one by a contemporary writer who reached the victorious army three weeks after it had taken the great fortress and two by authors writing a century after the event. From these records it seems that the siege began from the south on the morning of March 3, 1271. The little town outside the castle walls was quickly overrun, but heavy rains held up further attack for nearly three weeks. Then the outwork on the triangular plateau beyond the south wall of the fortress was easily taken. At this point the siege began in earnest, and after heavy mining, the great south-west tower of the outer enceinte collapsed and the attackers rushed in to find themselves confronted with the huge and impenetrable inner defences. These, however, were not put to the test, for the sultan resorted to trickery. Perhaps by means of a carrier pigeon, he sent a forged letter into the castle, apparently from the grand master of the Hospitallers, ordering the defenders to surrender since no help could be sent to them. This order was obeyed by the castellan, either because he thought the letter was genuine, or because it afforded an honourable excuse for abandoning a hopeless struggle. After the castle's surrender, the garrison was allowed to evacuate the fortress with their possessions.

After his great victory, the sultan is reputed to have sent another letter, this time addressed to the grand master of the order himself. In it he is supposed to have said (among other things): 'May the Lord include thee amongst the number of those who do not struggle against their destiny, but who fear to offer resistance to the master of victory. We announce to thee what God has done for us.' What God had in fact done was to open the last defences of Outremer to Islam.

A general view of the courtyard showing the cloister of the great hall on the left, and the porch to the chapel and the chapel itself on the right-hand side of the picture.

CHAPTER 4

CHATEAU D'ANGERS

The castle at Angers, still one of the most impressive fortresses of medieval Europe, stands on a rock above a tributary of the River Loire, from which it dominates the centre of the town. After the sugar-candy pleasure palaces scattered along the valley of the Loire, it is a welcome change to discover this grim fortress uncompromisingly dedicated to the serious business of war. The castle's appearance has been lightened by the formal gardens laid out in the moat and inside the enceinte, but the mighty walls and massive towers still act as a forcible reminder of the castle's military function.

The site was first fortified by Fulk the Black, or Fulk Nerra (987–1040), the Count of Anjou and founder of the family known to later generations as the Devil's brood. The first castle at Angers may well have looked something like the stone keep still surviving at Langeais, one of the castles built by Fulk to consolidate his conquests. The present castle dates from the reign of Louis IX (St Louis) of France, who reigned from 1226 to 1270. The idea of a saint rebuilding the stronghold of a devil may be romantic, but not entirely inappropriate, for the refortification of this important strategic site followed the expulsion of the house of Anjou—represented by the Plantagenet King John of England—from their ancient territories. The struggle between the kings of France and the kings of England, who were also the heirs to great French fiefs, will shortly be outlined in Chapter 6 on Château Gaillard, whose fall marked the capture of Normandy. The loss of Anjou belongs to the same story of Anglo-French conflict, and the castle at Angers is another example of the way in which the great castles of the middle ages were again and again the foci of important historical or cultural events.

The castle was begun in 1228, when King Louis was only 14 and

Left, the south curtain wall at Angers. On the right is the second gate, which was originally approached by a ramp and drawbridge. The sternness of the towers is lightened by the banded effect produced by the different types of stone and by the subtle battering, which reaches almost halfway up the height of the towers.

Below, an aerial view of the castle from the south. The bridge over the moat to the main gateway is on the eastern wall.

the regency of France was in the capable hands of his mother, Blanche of Castile. It was completed about ten years later, five years after Louis had assumed full control of his kingdom. The king was canonised within thirty years of his death, yet his saintly virtues were very different from those of his conventionally pious rival, Henry III of England. Louis was the ideal medieval king; a moral and devout Christian who applied his love of justice and honour to the government of his kingdom. He did not hesitate to oppose the clergy if he thought their demands were unreasonable or their actions unjust, and his awareness of his royal dignity even led him to oppose the pope's treatment of Emperor Frederick II, branded by some contemporaries as the antichrist himself, as we shall see in the chapter on Castel del Monte. The life of this Christian monarch ended—appropriately—during the crusade of 1270, whose failure sealed the fate of Krak.

The castle at Angers is surrounded by a massive curtain wall, which follows the outline of an irregular pentagon. It was defended on all sides (except that facing the river) by seventeen great drum towers. The base of both wall and towers was protected by a vast battered plinth sloping from a point about halfway up the structure's present height down into the moat, which completed the line of defence around the whole enceinte on the river side. The wall and towers were built on solid rock, and this too has been scarped to follow the line of the plinth, so that no projection was left as a foothold for the attackers. The banded effect of the strata of slate, sandstone and granite to some extent enlivens the severe and forbidding aspect of the masonry, but there is no other form of decoration to lighten the grimness of the mighty defences. A single tower—the one at the northernmost point of the enceinte—still rises above the top of the wall, and so gives us some idea of the castle when all seventeen towers reached to this height. These were dismantled to the level of the wall-walk on the orders of King Henry III (who intended to destroy the whole structure) in the late 16th century, when the castle's possession was fiercely disputed during the wars of religion.

Today's visitor enters the fortress by walking over a drawbridge and through the main gate (defended by a turret) in the east curtain wall. The gatehouse itself is formed by two of the great wall towers, set close together; the same formation is repeated at the south-east corner of the enceinte, where a second bridge once led up to another gateway. (This gateway can still be seen.) Inside the walls, the courtyard is considerably higher than the surrounding terrain, so that the lower reaches of the curtain wall, heavily protected by the huge

The Tour du Moulin or Windmill Tower, which was the only one not dismantled in the demolition ordered by King Henry III in the 16th century. Originally all the towers were of this height and were probably covered in with conical roofs.

plinth already described, were almost impregnable. Most of the early buildings inside the walls have disappeared, but in the centre of the courtyard there still stands the 15th-century chapel built for Yolande, wife of Count Louis II. Its vaulting is among the finer examples of late Gothic work. Next to the chapel is the so-called *petit château* and the gatehouse of an earlier castle.

Undoubtedly, Angers' greatest treasure is the sequence of tapestries depicting the Apocalypse, which now hang in a special display gallery inside the castle walls. Tapestry became the standard type of decoration in rich men's houses, and as demand grew during the 14th century, the tapestry manufacturers and designers of northern France and Flanders acquired an ever-increasing mastery of their art. The inventory taken of the castle of Vincennes in the reign of King Charles V (1364–80) mentions some thirty sets of tapestries, mostly devoted to secular subjects (though one depicted the history of Judas Maccabeus). The favourite themes for wall hangings were the stories of great heroes of classical myths or chivalric romances. The Apocalypse was perhaps an unusual choice for the decorations of a castle hall, but there can be no doubt that these superb tapestries were commissioned by Louis I, Count of Anjou, for the castle at Angers, and were executed at the end of the 14th century.

Luckily we can reconstruct from surviving records the detailed history of this great work of art. Originally the series consisted of ninety horizontal panels, arranged in two rows one above the other, divided by seven vertical panels depicting seven worthies of the Church. The whole vast frieze was 470 feet long and about 18 feet deep; along the bottom ran a border depicting a flowery meadow and along the top another narrow frieze showing angels set among clouds in the sky. Between these symbolic representations of heaven and earth, St John's great vision unfolds itself. The panels' background colours are alternately red and blue, and on some can be seen the letters 'L', 'M' and 'Y', probably the initials of Louis, his wife Marie, and Yolande, the wife of Count Louis II.

The tapestries were produced in the Paris workshop of Nicholas Bataille, the most famous tapissier of the time, and woven from cartoons prepared by Hennequin of Bruges, a painter employed by Charles V, the count's brother. The subjects were taken from two illuminated manuscripts in the royal library, which were lent, according to a record made at the time, by the king to the count for work on the tapestries. (The manuscripts still survive, one in the Bibliothèque Nationale, Paris, and the other in the library at

Opposite, two panels of the Apocalypse tapestries. Top, St John the Divine (who appears in every scene) and the dragon who 'cast out of his mouth water as a flood . . .' (Revelation xii. 15).

Bottom, St John sees 'a beast rise up out of the sea having seven heads and ten horns, and upon his horns ten crowns; . . . and the dragon gave him his great authority. And they worshipped the dragon which gave power unto the beast, and they worshipped the beast.' (Revelation xiii. 1–4).

Cambrai.) Again from contemporary sources, we know that the painter received 50 francs for the cartoons and Bataille 3000 francs for the tapestries. This was not Bataille's first commission for the count since we know that a payment of 1000 francs was made to him for the tapestries on the History of Hector of Troy, but it is unlikely that any of his other work equalled the splendour of the Apocalypse series. The tapestry is worked in wool, and the treatment of the subject is restrained, even austere; all subsidiary figures are rigidly excluded and the sense of drama is further heightened by the angular lines and limited use of colour—only thirty dyes are used in the whole vast work. Even today, when the colours have faded and the surviving seventy sections have been considerably, if expertly, restored, the impact is still tremendous.

The subsequent history of the tapestries is remarkable. When Louis I died in 1384, only thirty out of the ninety panels had been completed; the remaining two-thirds of the work was finished in the time of his son and successor Louis II, whose widow bequeathed it to their son René. On his death in 1480, the tapestries were removed to the cathedral of Angers where they hung for about 250 years. In the mid-18th century, when fashionable taste had rejected the art of the middle ages as barbaric and 'Gothic', the cathedral was cleared of its ancient treasures to make room for decorations in a more elegant and up-to-date style. The Apocalypse tapestries, with many other superb pieces, were put up for auction, but failed to find a buyer. For nearly a century, the dismantled sections of this great masterpiece mouldered in obscurity; some were cut up for floor rugs, and one large section was even used to protect orange trees in a greenhouse from the cold. In the 1840s, when Europe was rediscovering the glories of medieval art, the decayed tapestry fragments were bought for 300 francs by a devoted scholar and eventually, after much patient and skilful restoration, returned to the cathedral. After the Second World War, they were finally restored to the castle, where they were hung in the gallery designed especially for them.

The more we study the great castles of medieval Europe and the lives of the people who built them and lived in them, the more we become aware of the intricate political network, represented by Europe's powerful ruling families, that linked the histories of the lands of Christendom from Syria to Wales. Anjou, wrested from the Angevin kings of England by Philip Augustus of France, was bequeathed to Philip's grandson Charles, younger brother of St Louis, who built the castle of Angers. After complicated political negotiations,

106

Above, the chapel and ornamental gardens inside the curtain wall at Angers; to the left is the châtelet, *the gatehouse to the gardens built by King René in the 15th century.*

Right, the main gatehouse at Angers showing the stone bridge across the moat and the drawbridge. To the right is the Tour du Moulin, which originally housed a windmill—a common and necessary feature of a large medieval castle.

Left, three panels from the Apocalypse tapestries. Top, St John witnesses the descent of the great star known as Wormwood, which will turn the waters of the earth so bitter that men who drink them will die. 'And the third angel sounded and there fell a great star from heaven, burning as it were a lamp . . .' (Revelation viii. 10).

Centre, 'the army of horsemen . . . having breastplates of fire and of jacinth, and brimstone; and the heads of the horses were as the heads of lions . . . and their tails were like unto serpents.' (Revelation ix. 17).

Bottom, 'seven angels having [the vials of] the seven last plagues . . . and them that had gotten the victory over the beast . . . Stand on the sea of glass, having the harps of God.' (Revelation xv, 1 and 2).

Charles was adopted as the papal candidate for the throne of Sicily, occupied at the time by the heir to the Emperor Frederick II, the arch-enemy of the papacy, whom the pope was determined to dislodge. Charles of Anjou, reluctantly supported by his brother the French king, thereupon conquered the kingdom of Naples and Sicily and bequeathed the throne to his heirs. In Naples, the Castel Nuovo still stands as a memorial to his successful search for glory, and its sturdy towers and massive curtain wall are highly reminiscent of the castle of Angers, the capital of the new king's native province.

The Angevin dynasty founded by Charles continued to rule Naples until the expulsion of René the Good in 1435. René then returned to his birthplace, the Château of Angers, and there established a brilliant court. His patronage of poets and artists, his own literary efforts and his knightly virtues gained him a wide European reputation and have left a brilliant aura around his name. On his retirement to Provence in 1473, the last great chapter in the history of the castle of Angers was over, and on his death in 1480 it was annexed by the French crown.

Above, the Castle Nuovo at Naples, built in the 13th century for Charles of Anjou, King of Sicily. The stern, round towers with battering extending to the foundation rock suggest that the royal builder recalled the castle of his French capital when approving the plans for this fortress in his Italian kingdom.

Above left, the moat along the eastern wall at Angers with the bridge to the main gatehouse. Elsewhere the floor of the moat is laid out with ornamental gardens, but here it has been left wild for the castle deer, which graze off the brushwood. 109

CHAPTER 5

WELSH CASTLES

Caernarvon Castle stands on a tongue of flat land at the junction of the River Seiont with the Menai Strait; the little River Cadnant, which provided the castle and its walled borough with a third water boundary to the north, is now built over. From most vantage points the mighty fortifications are an impressive sight, but perhaps the castle's strength and splendour is best seen from the bank across the Seiont —the view illustrated in a watercolour by the 18th-century artist William Pars. Strategically, the castle is one link in the chain of fortifications encircling Snowdonia built by King Edward I as part of his campaign to conquer Wales. But as we shall see, Caernarvon was not only a fortress; it was also designed to house the offices of the new English administration in Wales—in short, to be the capital to the new Principality. Even so, the main purpose of the great Edwardian fortresses was military, and their design was dictated by considerations of defensive strength. This design, like that of so many European castles, was influenced by impressions brought back from the Levant, which Edward visited during the crusade of 1270.

Unlike most other medieval fortifications, we know a good deal about the men who built the Edwardian castles in Wales. The most important of these was the Savoyard, James St George, whose career in the service of the English king has already been outlined in the introduction. As was said before, James seems to have been a personal friend of the king—a friendship that is hardly surprising when we remember that Edward himself probably took a major hand in the design of the castles.

While not as intimidating as Conway, nor as wildly or romantically placed as Harlech, nor as perfect a text-book model as Beaumaris, Caernarvon can still claim to be the most imperious and magnificent

Above, a view of Caernarvon from across the River Seiont that gives a fine impression of the extent and majesty of the circuit of the curtain walls with their many towers. The stone revetment containing the motte of the earlier Norman castle can be seen projecting beyond the line of the wall to the right of the picture.

Right, Conway Castle, begun under the architect James St George in 1283, seen from the south across the River Gyffin. Originally the walls, like those of many other castles, would have been whitewashed. The tower in the centre shows the slight battering characteristic of many of the castle's towers, while that to the right is defended by a glacis.

of this group of castles. Its most distinctive feature is the unusual polygonal plan of its towers—a peculiarity also found in St George's castle of d'Esperance and possibly intended to mark Caernarvon from the beginning as the principal fortress of Wales. The living rooms in the towers—particularly those in the Eagle Tower—are spacious and stately, and inside the enceinte were the great hall, kitchens and apartments for the use of the royal household.

Caernarvon was designed with two main gates: the King's Gate on the town side, and the Queen's Gate in the south-east corner of the enceinte, looking towards the River Seiont. The eastern, or upper, ward surrounds the site of the motte belonging to the earlier Norman motte-and-bailey castle built by Hugh of Avranches, Earl of Chester, in the 11th century. For this reason, the Queen's Gate breaks the curtain wall high above the modern street level, and so provides one of the most impressive sights in the whole series of the Welsh castles. Like the main entrance at Conway, it was meant to be approached along a long ramp linked to the gateway by a turning bridge. From the wooden platform, the visitor can inspect the defensive armoury of the gate, the towers projecting on either side, the machicolations (or murder holes) above the entrance and the pivot bearings and pit for the manoeuvres of the turning bridge. The original plan of the gatehouse was never completed, and we cannot even be sure that the ramp itself was ever built.

The main entrance to the castle was through the King's Gate, where the precautions against attack, again not fully completed, were considerably more elaborate. As pointed out in the introduction, the defence of the entrance placed considerable demands on the ingenuity of the medieval military architect; Caernarvon is a striking example of the exercise of this ingenuity. After crossing the outer drawbridge, the attacker had to penetrate a succession of no fewer than five doors

Above, Harlech Castle, one of the four great Edwardian fortresses, from the south; originally the sea washed the foot of the rocky hill on which it stands. It was begun under the direction of St George about 1285 on a concentric plan; the low walls of the outer curtain are so close to those of the inner that the attackers could be engaged from both levels at once.

Right, a sketch plan of Caernarvon Castle. Originally the castle was divided at the narrow waist between the King's Gate and the Chamberlain's Tower into two wards.

Right, an aerial photograph of the castle at Caernarvon, which also shows the full circuit of the walls of the Edwardian borough. From above, one can clearly see the hour-glass shape of the fortress.

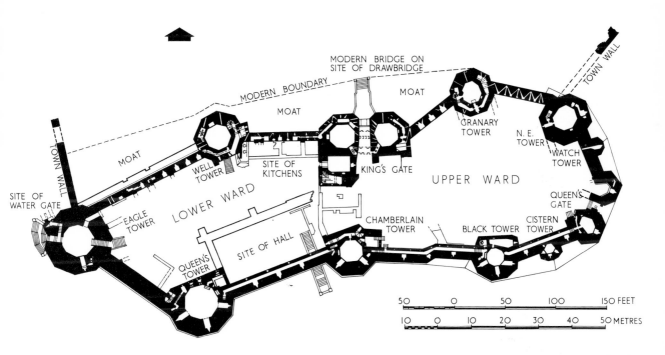

MODERN BRIDGE ON
SITE OF DRAWBRIDGE

MODERN BOUNDARY

MOAT

MOAT

MOAT

TOWN WALL

GRANARY
TOWER

N. E.
TOWER

WELL
TOWER

SITE OF
KITCHENS

KING'S GATE

UPPER WARD

WATCH
TOWER

TOWN WALL

SITE OF
WATER GATE

EAGLE
TOWER

LOWER WARD

QUEEN'S
TOWER

SITE OF HALL

CHAMBERLAIN
TOWER

BLACK TOWER

CISTERN
TOWER

QUEEN'S
GATE

| 50 | 0 | 50 | 100 | 150 FEET |

| 10 | 0 | 10 | 20 | 30 | 40 | 50 METRES |

Above, the Eagle Tower at Caernarvon with its three hexagonal turrets and the steps of the water gate at the foot; the town wall leads off to the left of the picture. The large handsome windows of the constable's lodgings are in striking contrast to the windows in the Wall Tower on the left.

Little is left of the elaborate works within the King's Gateway and indeed the hall above the gate itself was never completed. However, from the picture, left, the intended scale of the hall can be appreciated and the elegant mullioned window is typical of the spacious main rooms of great medieval castles.

and six portcullises, and pass over a second drawbridge, all the time exposed to defensive fire from arrow loops and machicolations. As at Harlech and Ghent, the chapel above the entrance passage was used for defence, two of the portcullises rose through its floor.

The next most important structure in the outer line of defences is the Eagle Tower. Almost certainly it was intended to be the residence of the king's lieutenant at Caernarvon, Sir Otto de Grandson, the first justiciar of North Wales and a Savoyard like the castle's architect. It was so-called from very early times because each of its three turrets was decorated with a stone eagle (the one on the west turret can still be seen), which probably derived from the eagle on the justiciar's coat of arms. This cluster of tall, polygonal watch towers rising from a single tower is unique; indeed, in every way the tower was a worthy home for its distinguished occupant. It has three storeys above ground level, each containing a spacious central room and well equipped with such side chambers in the walls as a kitchen, a small chapel and privies. The basement room led out through a gate and portcullis to the waterfront on the Menai Strait, and was to have been defended by a water gate. This might have been used as an entrance by high-ranking visitors arriving by water; a second water entrance at the foot of the Well Tower (the one immediately to the west of the King's Gate) was probably intended to take in supplies for the kitchens. These adjoined the north side of the Well Tower, and then ran along the inside of the curtain to the south tower of the King's Gate. Evidence shows that the kitchens were originally meant

Left, the principal apartment of the constable's lodgings in the Eagle Tower. The floor and ceiling timbers are modern, but the fireplace is original and its hooded chimney breast is typical of the period; the opening on the left leads to a small octagonal chapel.

to be built in stone, but that they were in fact completed in wattle and timber. Across the courtyard from the kitchens was the great hall of the castle. Only its foundations survive, but the magnificent ruins of the hall at Conway perhaps give some idea of its former size and grandeur. The original plan provided for another hall above the gatehouse, and the tower rooms and windows and window-seats of the incomplete building can still be seen.

Caernarvon's importance as an administrative centre and royal residence is reflected in the names of the Chamberlain, or Records, Tower and the Queen's Tower. The ample and spacious tower rooms, containing handsome fireplaces and separate sanitary facilities, and the buildings within the wards were designed to house the officials administering the Principality and to accommodate the royal household whenever the king visited his lands in Wales. It did not fulfil this purpose for long; two generations after the castle was built, it was being used mainly as a storage depot for arms and building materials. Even the most famous event in Caernarvon's history—the birth of Edward II, the first English Prince of Wales—must have taken place at a time when most of the existing building was still incomplete; the young prince, born on Welsh soil and—as his father promised the Welsh—unable to speak a word of English, first saw the light of day in the temporary half-timbered buildings put up for the visit of Edward I in 1284, the year after the castle was begun.

The building of the Welsh castles of Edward I is an important landmark in the history of medieval architecture. Not only are the structure of the great four—Conway, Beaumaris, Caernarvon and Harlech—among the finest surviving examples of the castle builder's art, but the whole series (which includes Flint and Rhuddlan) expresses the successful efforts of the most powerful and most centralised administration in Europe to carry out a coherent system of military and political rule. The castles were not the first Anglo-Norman fortifications in Wales nor the only ones built during this period (the great castle at Caerphilly was going up at the same time), but, unlike the others, they form a unified group, planned by one ruler as part of a deliberate policy for containing one particular area —Snowdonia—and almost entirely designed by one architect, James St George. It is rare to find such a clear expression of warfare, politics and even social administration in the monuments of the past; let us therefore take a brief look at the events that led up to their building.

Even before the Norman conquest of England, the Welsh and the English had been at odds. The new French rulers of England took up

The arrival of the Earl of Salisbury at the castle of Conway from an early 15th-century French manuscript. Even this stylised representation of the castle shows the characteristic shape of the great hall with its 'elbow bend'.

the old quarrels, which were mainly fought out between the Welsh princes and the Norman lords of the Marches until, in the 13th century, the domination of the anglophil Lord Rhys in the south yielded to that of the fiercely nationalist rule of Llewellyn the Great. His successes against the Normans were drastically curtailed at the Peace of Woodstock in 1247 between his descendant Llewellyn ap Gruffydd and Henry III of England, yet by 1258 the young Llewellyn had not only established his position in Wales but felt strong enough to assume the title of 'Prince of Wales'; by 1263 he had also recovered large areas of Welsh territory from the English. By the Treaty of Montgomery in 1267 between Henry and Llewellyn, the English king acknowledged many of the Welsh ruler's claims, including that to the title of Prince of Wales on payment of a heavy fine. But the situation

The view, left, inside the walls of Caernarvon looking away from the Eagle Tower shows the stone foundations for the kitchens on the left and for the great hall on the right.

Below, an engraving by J. Boydell, published in 1750, shows that the town of Caernarvon had only just begun to spread beyond the confines of its medieval walls. The vale of the Cadnant (now built over) is hidden behind the houses in the foreground.

soon deteriorated again when an English judicial commission was appointed for Wales and Llewellyn found himself pressed for payment, even though the Marcher lords were in fact encroaching on the authority of the title for which he was paying. Finally he was summoned to pay homage to the new King Edward I on terms that he considered humiliating. Llewellyn, like his predecessors, recognised the feudal suzerainty of the English kings, but regarded himself free to administer his land and his vassals without interference; he certainly rejected the validity of English law and custom in Wales. Ironically, his feudal relationship to the English crown was very similar to that of the kings of England, as claimants to French territories, to the crown of France.

Not surprisingly, the English took a rather different view of the Welsh situation than they did of the French. So when Llewellyn, after what Edward considered to be ample notice, refused to pay homage until the Welsh grievances were dealt with, the king 'went upon him as a rebel and a disturber of the king's peace'. The ensuing war ended in 1277 in the humiliating Treaty of Conway, by which Llewellyn retained the title of Prince of Wales, but had his territories reduced to those of Gwynedd, or modern Snowdonia. The English owed their victory not only to their ability to find Welsh allies, but, more important, to a series of aggressive and efficient sea attacks along the coast of Wales. This triumph consolidated English supremacy in Wales, and Edward proceeded to embark on the vast and costly programme of building described in this chapter. The major castles, together with the walls of the new boroughs established as centres of the English administrative network, formed an integrated system of defence containing the once mighty Welsh prince in his mountain stronghold. Inevitably Llewellyn, aided by his brother David, attempted to break the stranglehold, but in 1283 the Welsh princes were finally defeated and Snowdonia fell into English hands. In the following year, the new prince was born at Caernarvon and the story seemed over. But the final chapter only came eleven years later with the widespread revolt led by Madog ap Llewellyn. This time even the great (though unfinished) fortress of Caernarvon failed to stand up to the fury of the Welsh. The castle was taken, and the sheriff slain inside the walls, although by March the revolt was ended by the defeat of Madog on the field of Maes Moydog. Caernarvon was rebuilt, and the new castle of Beaumaris at the other end of the strait begun. From then on, North Wales was to remain under English rule with the great stone walls as a perpetual grim reminder of Welsh defeat.

CHAPTER 6

CHATEAU GAILLARD

Château Gaillard, one of the most famous and also one of the most complex examples of medieval architecture, stands in a break in the wide sweeping chalk cliffs on the east bank of the Seine, a few miles above its junction with the River Eur. It rises above the river and the little town of Les Andeleys, dominating both from the massive rock on which it is built. From below, the castle seems almost inaccessible; the visitor approaches it by climbing a winding road that swings round behind the castle until he eventually reaches the great bastion that had appeared so remote from the valley. Yet only from this vantage point does the visitor realise the full strategic value of the site, for the rock is surrounded by steep ravines, so that the castle stands on the central plateau in a naturally defensible position.

The castle was built by Richard the Lionheart, who in 1189 inherited the whole of the vast Angevin Empire, comprising not only the kingdom of England, the duchies of Normandy and Aquitaine and the county of Anjou, but claims to other territories in France and to Wales and Ireland. Yet the administration of his lands occupied little of Richard's short reign. He was, to quote Sir Steven Runciman, 'a bad son, a bad husband and bad king, but a gallant and splendid soldier'. His reputation as a soldier was confirmed during the Third Crusade, but on his return to Europe in 1192 he continued to exercise his military skill against his former crusader ally, King Philip Augustus of France, in the recurring Anglo-French conflict over English claims in France.

The success of Richard's campaign against the French largely depended on the castles of Normandy, of which Château Gaillard, built to defend the eastern approaches to Normandy, was of crucial strategic importance. The castle was begun in 1196 and completed

Opposite, Château Gaillard from the west—a view that gives some idea of the strength of the site and the precipitous ravines that surround it.

121

probably three years later. Richard himself certainly had a considerable hand in the design of the castle, which is obviously influenced by his experience of crusader castles. He was delighted with it when it was completed, and named it his 'Saucy Castle'—Château Gaillard.

The Saucy Castle was built as a gesture of defiance against the French king, whose annexations of English territory were largely recovered by Richard; it was also begun in defiance of the Church. As was pointed out in the introduction, the building of a castle often conflicted with local interests and territorial rights. In this instance, the superb military site chosen by Richard was in the domain of Walter of Coutances, the Archbishop of Rouen. Ignoring this fact, Richard began building; when protests followed, he ignored them too and carried on the work. The archbishop put the whole duchy under interdict and, according to legend, divine displeasure showed itself in the form of a rain of blood. Yet, it was said, even if an angel had descended to command the king to stay his hand, he would merely have been greeted with a curse. A year after the castle was begun, however, the king and the archbishop came to terms on payment of generous compensation by Richard.

Gaillard was defended not only by the fortifications on the rock itself but also by an elaborate system of outworks (which are no longer visible) and a new, fortified town, of which Les Andeleys is the modern descendant. The Seine and its little tributary formed the basis of the outer defences. The two branches of the tributary meet just above its junction with the Seine, and the new town was built across the single stream with a system of dams on the east side and channels to north and south, which together formed an artificial lake to the east of the town. The main works on the Seine itself consisted of a tower on the little island of Andeley, which controlled a barrage linking the island with the two river banks. Upstream, opposite the castle itself, a stockade of stakes in the river-bed also helped to impede any enemy ships that might try to combine with forces attacking from the land. In time of peace, these barriers were of course open, but the castle's commander imposed tolls on all shipping passing through them. This levy, combined with the large tracts of land belonging to the castle, were an important source of the income needed to maintain the garrison. As for the new town, it was heavily fortified with towers and walls, and its street plan, like that of many towns laid out in the middle ages, was largely geometric. To persuade people to settle in the new borough, the king sold the free burgage (citizenship) with its accompanying privileges for five shill-

122

Right, the view from the castle of the little town of Les Andeleys below. The island was an important part of the outer defences of the fortress.

A sketch plan of Château Gaillard. The ground falls away steeply on all sides of the middle bailey, and an attacking force had to win the outer bailey before it could attack the main stronghold.

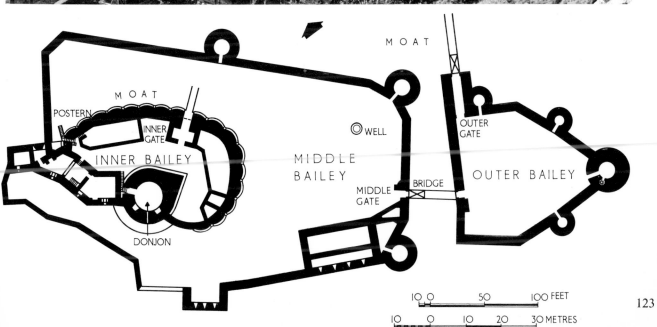

MOAT

POSTERN

MOAT

INNER GATE

INNER BAILEY

WELL

OUTER GATE

MIDDLE BAILEY

OUTER BAILEY

DONJON

MIDDLE GATE

BRIDGE

10 0   50   100 FEET

10   0   10   20   30 METRES

Above, a view of the castle from across the river shows the drama of its commanding site to full advantage. A castle's effectiveness was greatly affected by its position, and a fine military architect such as Richard I must have been delighted with the possibilities of such a site.

Left, the site of Château Gaillard, which should be compared with the plan on p. 123. The wall of the inner bailey and the great donjon are comparatively well preserved, but only fragments of the middle bailey survive. At the top of the picture can be seen the main tower and part of the wall of the outer bailey.

ings. All in all, the establishment of a major new fortress with its surrounding defences, including a fortified town and the provision of lands for the upkeep of the garrison, was a massive undertaking. But the whole complex depended ultimately on the castle itself, on which we must now concentrate our attention.

We know the names of the three chief clerks of the works at Andeley and its castle: Sawale, son of Henry, Robert, son of Hermer, and Mathew, son of Ernard. How much part they played in the building of the castle is unknown, but, as was said earlier, it can be assumed that the design of the fortress was largely Richard's inspiration. It stands on a plateau about 600 feet long by about 200 feet at its widest point, almost entirely surrounded by ravines of varying steepness. One of the builders' first tasks was to make these natural obstacles even deeper by digging. Yet even when this was done, some parts of the site were still much more open to attack than others. The castle itself was thus designed to compensate for these differences.

The basic design of the castle consists of a line of three baileys; the keep was built at the most inaccessible point of the third bailey—the one most distant from the attacker. Because of the lie of the land, any attack must, almost of necessity, follow the line of the defences, taking each bailey in turn before attempting the final assault on the keep. The conventional idea of a bailey castle has however been modified at Gaillard, whose complex of middle bailey, inner bailey and keep represents an early European example of a concentric castle. This layout may well have been the fruit of Richard's observations in the Middle East. Another feature, which became increasingly common in later castles, was the rounded contour of the wall towers and of the keep itself. To reach the garrison's last stronghold, the besiegers were confronted with three ditches crossed by drawbridges and complex masonry barriers, which combined to make the fortress almost impregnable. As we shall see later, the fall of Château Gaillard was brought about by the quick wits of its attackers and not by the weakness of its defences.

The curtain walls of the outer and middle baileys followed the contours of the plateau and were reinforced by round towers. The curtain of the inner bailey was also protected not only by hollows in the land but by a highly unusual corrugated surface, of which almost every inch could be protected by covering fire. Perhaps the most remarkable part of the whole structure is the keep, whose walls are massively thickened where it juts out towards the line of attack. This, combined with the sharply battered base, made mining extremely

A detailed view of the keep and the inner bailey illustrating the strange 'corrugated' nature of the curtain wall in this part of the castle.

125

difficult and also tended to deflect the weapons of the enemy artillery. The unusual inverted buttresses were probably meant to support a system of stone machicolations, which would have been rare at so early a date. In fact, the whole of this part of the castle may never have been completed. The English authority on castles, Mr Sidney Toy, points out that the detailed record of the siege by William of Brittany contains no mention of an attack on the keep. And since the garrison defended the castle with the utmost resolution and courage, he convincingly argues that it is unlikely that they would have surrendered if the keep had been in a defensible state.

Richard died in 1199 and two years later King Philip renewed his campaign to capture Normandy from John (Richard's successor). In the summer of 1203, Philip decided to lay siege to Château Gaillard and so capture the key to the duchy. To modern eyes, as to those of contemporaries, the attempt seems astonishing. Yet it is possible to trace the siege stage by stage from the account left by the French chronicler William of Brittany.

The Norman castles were largely garrisoned by mercenaries: Welsh, Brabançon, Gascon and possibly even Saracen. The garrison at Château Gaillard, however, under the command of the Constable of Chester, Roger de Lacy, was largely English, loyal and well provisioned to withstand a long siege. King John returned to England confident that the mighty fortress would hold out well into the following spring and so give him the time to collect the reinforcements he so badly needed. His hopes seemed reasonable, but, as so often in medieval sieges, the fate of the castle was decided by other than purely military factors.

In August, Philip attacked the town and the river works, which, because of the shortage of manpower, had to be surrendered after a month. The siege of the castle then began. Recognising the castle's formidable defensive position, Philip put up elaborate counterworks around the castle (to prevent any attempt at sortie), and settled down to starve out the defenders. The peninsula, formed by the two rivers on which Gaillard stood, was cut by a double trench controlled by walls and wooden towers equipped with drawbridges. The besieging forces were out of bow shot from the castle; the fortress and its defenders, unable to retaliate, were therefore condemned to inactivity. As the winter dragged on, the morale of the garrison might be expected to suffer, whereas the confidence of the French was unshaken. The chronicler even records the songs of the French soldiers, referring to the castle as 'an eyrie overcrowded with fledglings, which

The keep at Château Gaillard, showing the steep battering of the walls and the buttresses, which may have been designed to carry stone machicolations. As can be seen on p. 124, the keep projects beyond the curtain wall of the inner bailey out to the edge of the precipitous cliff on which the castle was built. Here natural defences made machicolations unnecessary and also permitted large unprotected windows.

will have to turn out in the spring'. And the eyrie was indeed over-crowded. The garrison was well provided with food and drink for a long siege, but as well as the garrison of about 300 men, there were at least 1500 civilians from Les Andeleys. After two months, de Lacy decided to expel some of his fledglings; about 500 of the oldest and weakest were sent out of the castle and let through the French lines. They were followed a few days later by another 500, but a third party was turned back on the orders of King Philip. They returned to the castle, only to find the gates locked against them.

For the next three months, these people lived in the surrounding ravines, enduring the crossfire of the combatants and scratching for any miserable vegetation that could be found. The few survivors were reduced to cannibalism, and when King Philip returned to conduct the final stages of the siege, he was apparently so shocked by their plight that he ordered that they should be fed. Almost all died as their weakened digestions succumbed to their first heavy meal.

At the end of February, spurred on by John's expected arrival in the spring, Philip decided to attack the castle. Petrariae were trained on the south-east wall of the outer bailey and a covered gallery built from the French line to the edge of the ditch, which it was planned to fill. The whole operation was covered from a belfry wheeled up to the edge of the ditch. It was slow work, however, and, according to the chronicler, the troops eventually lost patience and climbed up their

Above, another view from Château Gaillard, looking out over the river. The picture also shows the method of building: flint rubble core contained by a brick or stone facing. This technique was commonly used for large medieval buildings.

Opposite, a close-up of the smaller outer tower, which was connected with the inner bailey by a passage. The tower would have been used primarily as a lookout post.

129

scaling ladders from the unfilled ditch to the base of the main round tower of the outer bailey. Here sappers were able to undermine the foundations of the tower. On its collapse, the garrison withdrew.

But Gaillard was built to resist capture, and after five months the French had only reached the second line of defence. Here they were confronted with another and more formidable ditch, and then beyond it the central citadel. Ironically, at this stage King John was indirectly defeated by his own hand. Among his improvements to the great castle was a group of buildings in the middle bailey, surrounded by a wall overlooking the ditch dividing it from the outer bailey. Unfortunately for John, high up in the wall of the new building was an unbarred window. This was spotted by one of the French soldiers preparing for this second and more concentrated assault. This soldier, whose name was Peter the Snub Nose, persuaded a group of friends to follow him down into the moat. There they searched the base of the main walls for the discharge points of the castle drains. They then climbed up the drains to a point just below the window, through which they broke into the room beyond. (Incidentally, the drains at Conway, built a century later, were constructed in such a way that entry was impossible.) Once inside, Peter and his men boldly hammered on the locked door, shouting out to one another to give the impression that large numbers of enemy troops had broken in. Surprisingly, the ruse worked, and the defenders decided that the simplest way to meet this unexpected and unmeasured threat was to set fire to the buildings. But luck was against them, and the fire swept across the whole enclosure. While the defenders were withdrawing to the inner bailey, the French managed to beat their way out of the building and opened the gates to their comrades.

The siege now reached its last desperate phase. Yet even at this stage, the determined garrison, though reduced to 180 effective fighting men, might have held out in the main citadel if the bridge leading into the inner bailey had not been built on a tongue of solid rock. This gave the attackers a firm base for their next operation, which was to send over a cat, or mobile penthouse, to cover the mining of the main gate. The miners were forced to retreat by an English countermine, but the wall, weakened by mining from both sides, collapsed under the attack of the petrariae. The long siege was over. The garrison, reduced to 36 knights and 120 men, still refused to surrender and was taken prisoner. The Saucy Castle had at last been humbled and its fall marked the loss of the Duchy of Normandy to the English crown for ever.

CHAPTER 7

THE ALHAMBRA

Al-Qal' al-Hamra, the Red Fortress, dominates the town of Granada from one of the last spurs of the Sierra Nevada as it thrusts northwards into the plains of Andalusia. Its walls contain the castle and the palace of the rulers of the kingdom of Granada, the last Muslim state in the Iberian peninsula. For, like many of the castles studied in this book, the Alhambra began its career as a stronghold and later developed into a stately residence: the humble hill-fort became a great palace. No other castle in Europe achieved the richness of this luxurious pleasure seat in its wooded parks; yet in the year of the eventual defeat of its Arab lords, the Alhambra (with the town of Granada) withstood an eight-month siege, and its fall was a fitting end to the glories of the seven centuries of Islamic Spain. The

The Alhambra from the north-east; from outside the walls the fortress presents a forbidding aspect. In the centre is the Tower of the Comares (also called the Tower of the Ambassadors), while to the right can be seen the Tower of Homage and the other main tower of the east fortifications of the old alcazaba.

Christian conquerors built their own residence on the site, but here we are only concerned with the Islamic and not with the later palace built by the Emperor Charles V.

One of the great themes of medieval history is provided by the conflicts and contacts between the two great religious civilisations of Islam and Christendom. The frontier ran from the Levant, through southern Italy and Sicily to Spain. In all these areas the hostile civilisations were influenced by each other; in the crusader states of Outremer, Frankish society took on an Oriental flavour that shocked its European visitors; in southern Italy the court of the Emperor Frederick II derived its exotic character from a blend of European, Byzantine and Arab culture, while in Spain the legacy of the Muslim centuries is still widely felt today. The crusades represented the most dramatic Christian counterattack, but the reconquest of Spain and Portugal was a slow, continuous process that lasted seven centuries and only ended with the conquest of Granada in 1492. Cultural contacts across the fluctuating battle line were a source of enrichment to European civilisation as a whole, while the battle between the two creeds produced two distinct minority groups: the Mozarabs, the Christians inside Islam, and the Mudejars, the Muslims inside Christendom. Yet by the end of the middle ages, the two religious civilisations had retreated behind what today would seem to be their inevitable geographical boundaries: the Strait of Gibraltar to the south and the Mediterranean coastline to the east. The Alhambra, like Krak, belongs to this story of mutual withdrawal.

The site had been fortified since the ninth century, but it was during the reign of Mohammed I of Granada that it acquired real importance. Mohammed was the son of one of the genuinely Arab families that had been subjects of the Berber dynasty of the Almohades; the crumbling of their power, weakened from within by misgovernment and from without by the attacks from the Christian kingdoms of Spain and Portugal, threatened to extinguish Arab rule in the peninsula; and when Córdoba was captured by Ferdinand III of Aragon in 1236, the mightiest centre of Spanish Islam passed into Christian hands. At this point, the young Ibn Banu Nasr proclaimed himself Mohammed I of Granada, the only remaining Muslim state. The threat of further Christian advance made the fortification of the frontiers absolutely necessary, and his reign saw the building and refortification of several fortresses, of which the Alcazaba at Malaga and the Alhambra at Granada are two of the best-known. The complex of buildings inside its containing curtain wall known

Opposite, the Justice Gate of the Alhambra, Granada. Above the gate can be seen the talismanic open hand symbolising the five virtues of the Mohammedan faith.

Below, the pomegranate of Granada carved on a wall in the Alhambra. The fruit was the symbol of the kingdom, which derived its name from the Spanish word for pomegranate.

132

The sketch plan of the Alhambra, below, shows how the walls of the alcazaba or fortress to the south-west were extended to comprise a large fortified area enclosing the palatial residence of the rulers of Granada.

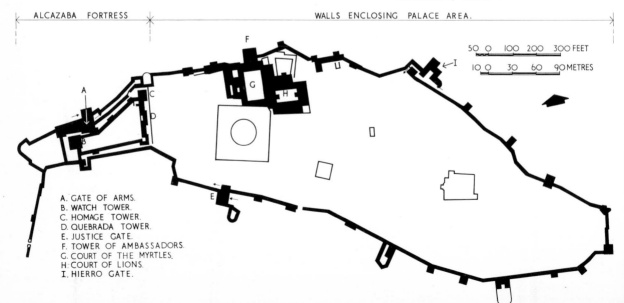

ALCAZABA FORTRESS

WALLS ENCLOSING PALACE AREA.

50 0   100 200 300 FEET

10 0   30   60   90 METRES

A. GATE OF ARMS.
B. WATCH TOWER.
C. HOMAGE TOWER.
D. QUEBRADA TOWER.
E. JUSTICE GATE.
F. TOWER OF AMBASSADORS.
G. COURT OF THE MYRTLES.
H. COURT OF LIONS.
I. HIERRO GATE.

comprehensively as the Alhambra is the product of centuries of building. Most of the Moorish work dates from the reigns of Mohammed I and his successors Mohammed II (1273–1302), Yusuf I (1333–54) and Mohammed V (1362–91). The walls enclose a long narrow area, some 800 yards at its longest point and about 230 yards at its widest; in the north-west tip of the enclosure is the alcazaba, or fortress, and we must now look at this in some detail. The original structure of Mohammed I is contained by the inner wall, defended at its north-west extremity by the great square Bell (or Watch) Tower, which guarded the main entrance of the original castle. The south-east wall is protected by two rectangular towers, of which the northernmost Tower of Homage is perhaps the better known; an attack on this wall was further hampered by a ditch running along its whole length and separating it from the great palace area enclosed by the curtain walls. This 13th-century castle, the alcazaba, was further fortified with additional curtain walls in the 14th century, and later still with the curved extension to the walls at the extreme end of the whole enceinte; the shape of this later addition may, it has been suggested, have been designed to make it stronger and better able to deflect the new weapon, artillery, in use in the peninsula at least as early as the 1340s. The most impressive feature of these later additions is the gate known as the Puerta de las Armas, built during the reign of Yusuf I.

The gate projects at right-angles to the wall and the entrance is placed in the side of the Tower, so that an attacking force would have to approach it with the right, unshielded flank to the wall and thus exposed to the fire of the defenders. After two right-angled turns within the tower, the attackers would debouch into a narrow alley formed by the two outer walls of the defences; the next entrance is at the end of this alley and leads into the gate at the foot of the Homage Tower. Only when he had emerged from this circuitous and deadly route did the enemy gain the innermost line of the defences. The alcazaba was the strongest point of the whole defensive system, but the whole circuit of the walls was protected by a series of strong towers and gateways, which were added and improved upon by later kings. The Puerta de Hierro on the north-east wall was equipped with a barbican, which made it almost as forbidding an obstacle as the Puerta de las Armas, while the great Puerta de la Justitia is (like all the main gateways to the castle) a bent entrance, and is further strengthened by an additional tower. This Gate of Justice is today the main entrance to the Alhambra; it was built in the reign of Yusuf I

The first fortress of the Alhambra was only one of a number of similar castles built by the rulers of Granada to protect their territories from the Christian kingdoms of the north. The picture, opposite, shows the Tower and Gate of the Arches of the Alcazaba at Malaga.

Below, the former eastern outer wall of defences to the Alcazaba of Granada; it was protected by a ditch and by the two great towers of Quebrada (centre) and of Homage.

and derives its name from the fact that it is traditionally the site of the open-air court of justice of the Muslim rulers. In the keystone of the arch over the gateway is carved an open hand—a popular Islamic talisman.

Most of the vast fortifications we have described were built during the reign of Mohammed I, and according to tradition, were completed in a single year. Although we may allow the king's flatterers a certain licence, we can be sure that with the Christian enemies pressing on the frontiers of the little kingdom, the work was hurried through with the greatest possible speed.

Although the Alhambra was designed first and foremost as a fortress, it was also the chief residence of the kings of Granada. No account of it would be complete without mention of the rich and dazzling beauties of the patios, halls and towers that make up the magnificent Casa Real. These lie to the east of the alcazaba and are approached today by crossing the Machuca patio, since the original entrance area, patio and mosque have been destroyed. In the time of the Moorish kings, a visitor would have gone through these first courts and then entered the mexuar, or maswar, the audience area found at the entrance to most Arab royal residences. This led into the Cuarto Dorado and from there into the charming and stately Court of the Myrtles (in Spanish, the Patio de Arrayanes). The court,

Above, a view from the fortifications of the old alcazaba over the surrounding countryside. The Tower of Homage (centre) controls the gate into the inner courtyard, which is approached by the ramp between the inner and outer walls.

Above right, the Court of the Myrtles in the Alhambra, a superb combination of water, trees and stone, which was a characteristic feature of Moorish architecture in Spain. The Hall of the Ambassadors in the great square tower of the same name was approached through the anteroom leading off the court, the Sala de la Barca.

Opposite, the Court of the Myrtles seen from the entrance to the Sala de la Barca. The colonnades at both ends provide a pleasant shaded walk through the courtyard; in the centre of each side wall are entrances leading to other parts of the palace and to the rooms that line the court.

136

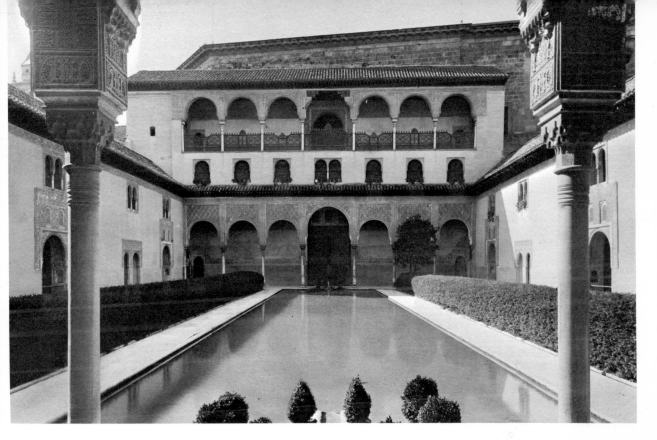

which runs at right-angles to the outer wall of the fortress, was the elegant forecourt to the great Hall of the Ambassadors in the Comares Tower, the main tower in the defences of the northern enceinte. Comares is probably the Spanish corruption of the Arabic word *qamariyya*—a style of coloured-glass windows first used in Cairo in the 13th century—and the elegant, yet now empty, window openings were almost certainly once glazed with richly coloured panes. Even without the vibrating colours of the original windows, the Hall of the Ambassadors is still the most magnificent as well as the largest room in the Alhambra; indeed it is one of the finest examples of medieval domestic architecture, either Muslim or Christian, to have survived. Inscriptions on the walls include the name of Yusuf I, during whose reign this great audience chamber was prepared; according to a contemporary account, the throne was placed here, and it would be hard to imagine a more fitting setting for great state receptions.

The Court of the Myrtles was one of the many exquisite additions to the Alhambra made by Mohammed V, who came to the throne eight years after the death of Yusuf. In the centre of the patio is an ornamental pond surrounded with myrtle trees; at either end is a porchway flanked by six colonnaded arches and at the southern end of the Court there is also a colonnaded balcony at first-floor level.

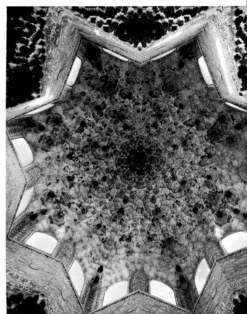

Behind the long, plain walls, each pierced by a central archway leading to the Cuarto Dorado to the west and the Royal Bath and Court
of the Lions to the east, are the living quarters. The whole ensemble
of the patio is a breathtaking example of the way in which the Moorish
architects of Andalusia managed, apparently without effort, to blend
the separate elements of water, vegetation and architecture into a
harmonious whole.

Behind the Court of the Myrtles are the private royal apartments,
the Court of the Lions, and leading off from it, the Hall of the Kings
(Sala de los Reyes), the Room of the Two Sisters (Sala de las dos
Hermanas) and the Room of the Abencerrajes. The Court of the
Lions, perhaps the most famous part of the whole Alhambra, derives
its name from the exquisite central fountain. This is in the form of an
alabaster basin supported by twelve marble lions, carved in a
brutally stylised manner that is a strong contrast to the delicate calm
of the surrounding courtyard. The court, which is 116 feet long by 66
feet wide, is paved with square, coloured tiles, surrounded by colonnades of 124 marble pillars and enlivened by rills of water and
ornamental trees. Like the court and its surrounding rooms and
138 vestibules, the exquisite Room of the Two Sisters was also built for

Mohammed V. The name derives from the two large marble slabs that form part of the pavement; above is a glorious honeycomb dome composed of more than 5000 cells and supported on superb stalactite vaulting—a typical feature of Mozarabic work. Beyond the Dos Hermanas is the charming little room called the Daraxa Mirador, which looks out on to the garden, while on the other side of the Court of the Lions is the Sala de los Abencerrajes with its magnificent roof.

Water is the secret of the Alhambra's charm; the play of light on the surfaces of the pools, the reflections scattered upon the surrounding walls and pillars and the sound of the fountain splashing in the sunlit courts gives the whole palace a feeling of gentle animation. Yet the rust-coloured, ore-bearing site—known to the Arabs as al-Sabika, 'the ingot'—was an arid, rocky spur admirable for defence but at first glance far from ideal as a site for a pleasure palace. As we have already pointed out, the Alhambra was originally designed as a castle, but behind the strong fortifications of the citadel, the kings of Granada were determined to build themselves a residence that was beautiful and comfortable as well as safe. The aqueduct built by Mohammed I not only brought water for the domestic needs of the garrison but for the decoration of the palace as it took shape inside the walls. A complex network of channels supplied the numerous privies and provided the necessary sanitation, usually so crude a feature of medieval domestic architecture.

In 1492, the Christian monarchs of Spain finally established their supremacy throughout the whole peninsula and in the same year the discoveries of Columbus dramatically widened the horizons of their power across the Atlantic. But the more important event to contemporaries was the completion of the reconquest of Spain, marked by the capture of the kingdom of Granada and symbolised by the fall of the capital and of the Alhambra. Thus the Red Fortress, established by the founder of the kingdom, fell with the kingdom. This new state had risen from the ruins of the former Almohad Empire as it collapsed under external attack and internal conflict; its own end was similar. Apart from renewed pressure from enemies to the north, Granada was torn by family rivalries. One of the most powerful of these families was the Abencerrajes, and the room in the Alhambra named after them is the traditional site of a banquet held for them by the last king of Granada, Boabdil. Having lured them under his roof, he slaughtered them in a desperate and brutal attempt to shore up the fabric of a state that shortly was to be destroyed from outside.

CHAPTER 8

CASTILIAN CASTLES

Among the territories of medieval Europe, Spain was particularly rich in castles; and of her provinces, Andalusia to the south and Castile to the north were especially well-endowed. Indeed, a book on castles of Europe would hardly be complete without mentioning an area that even derived its name—Castile—from the heavy concentration of fortresses inside its boundaries.

After the wave of Islamic conquest had swept northwards across the Iberian peninsula and into France during the eighth century, the only Christian territory that remained was the tiny kingdom of the Asturias along the north coast of Spain; from this base began the long process of reconquest that was to occupy the next seven hundred years. As the Christians pushed back the Arabs, new kingdoms crystallised. Among the most important of these was the kingdom of León (centred upon the town of that name), but by the middle of the 12th century the neighbouring country of Castile (with its capital at Burgos) had successfully established its hegemony, and from this period the destinies of Spain were closely linked with those of its ruling house. By the early 13th century, the kingdom of Castile, comprising the former territories of León, Asturias and Galicia, had pushed its frontiers past the whole length of the Douro river as far south as the Tagus; by the 1260s Christian rule extended to the south coast of the peninsula, leaving only the kingdom of Granada in Muslim hands. This process of reconquest, which viewed in the perspective of history appears as a single, massive wave of advance, was in fact punctuated by a series of advances and temporary retreats in the face of the infidel and by internecine warfare between the Christians themselves, largely caused by Castile's usurpation of León's position of leading state. In view of this perpetual turbulance and

A view of the famous Alcazar of Segovia from the valley to the north of the castle. The picture shows the termination of the spur of rock between the rivers Eresma and Clamores on which the fortress-palace is built.

warfare, it is hardly surprising that the strife-torn land of Spain is covered with castles of all descriptions. This chapter is concerned with four fortresses of Old Castile: the castle at Coca, the Castillo de la Mota at Medina del Campo, the castle at Peñafiel and the Alcazar at Segovia. Of these the Alcazar of Segovia is probably the most famous. It shares its name (from an Arabic word for fortress) with the great castles at Toledo and Seville; like them—and indeed much of the heritage of medieval Spain—it clearly shows the marks of Arab culture. Its external appearance resembles that of many Gothic castles in other parts of continental Europe, but the decoration inside is in the style known as mudéjar—that is, fashioned by Arab craftsmen who had adopted the religion of their conquerors. This great fortress-palace at Segovia stands on the rocky spur between the two rivers Eresma and Clamores, where it seems to sail the landscape like some mighty galleon with a sharply pointed prow formed by its wall and the Tower of John II as its poop.

The site may well have been the acropolis of some primitive, pre-Roman settlement, and on the arrival of the Romans themselves Segovia became an important town; the great aqueduct built by them is still used for bringing water to the city. The site was fortified under the Visigoths and was refortified during the 11th century by the rulers of the great Muslim caliphate of Córdoba as one of the many strongpoints set up to stem the tide of the Christian advance from the north. In 1083, however, Segovia finally passed into Christian hands when it was taken by the armies of Alfonso VI of León and Castile; two years later, this warrior-king captured Toledo, but his successes provoked a massive Arab counterattack during which some of his conquests were retaken. The fact that Segovia was not among them was perhaps partly the result of Alfonso's new fortifications on the site of the present castle. His great successor Alfonso X, surnamed the Wise, also added to the Alcazar at Segovia, but the fortress as we see it today owes its shape primarily to the 15th-century work carried out for John II and his son and successor, Henry IV. From the end of the 18th century onwards, the castle was used as an academy for students of artillery, but in 1862 it was gutted by fire and its fabric was not completely restored until the last quarter of the 19th century; today it houses military archives.

The Tower of John II. The decorative brickwork is a feature of the exterior of the Alcazar as a whole, while the hanging turrets are to be found in fortresses in other parts of Castile.

In the view of the Castel Coca, above, we can see how the later fortress rose on the foundations of the original 11th- and 12th-century castles. As at Segovia, the walls are protected by hanging turrets, but here this feature has been given very elaborate treatment.

As can be seen, left, the walls at Castel Coca are defended by strong corner towers and clustering turrets while the base is further strengthened by a steep batter. The brickwork has been used to full decorative effect but the circular gun ports and arrow loops underline the aggressive purpose of the building.

Left, the main square tower of the Castilo de la Mota at Medina built for King John II, and reminiscent of the tower added by him to the Alcazar at Segovia, though there the machicolations give added protection. Particularly interesting are the square holes evident on all the walls; these would have carried the beams supporting the scaffolding during building.

Below, the castle of Peñafiel, dating largely from the 14th century though the square keep that gives the castle its unique character was begun some 100 years later. Here, too, there are traces of the holes to receive scaffolding timbers, and an iron grille, another feature typical of medieval castles, which covers the outer window to prevent possible entry by the enemy.

145

The most arresting feature of the castle's exterior is the rectangular Tower of John II with the hanging turrets typical of this part of Spain. Inside, the rooms—for example, the Salon de la Galera with a mudejar frieze executed for Henry III's queen Catherine, daughter of John of Gaunt, the Salon del Trono and the Salon del Solio—tell the familiar story of transition form fortress to palace. From its early years until the reign of Philip II in the 16th century, the Alcazar at Segovia was a favourite residence of the rulers of Castile. In the 13th century, a session of the *Cortes* (the national legislature) was convened there by Alfonso X, whose legendary humiliation by the miraculous intervention of the Almighty is enshrined in the room known as the Pieza del Cordón. Puffed up, it is said, by pride in his own wisdom, Alfonso uttered the heretical statement that, if he had been in charge, the universe would have been ordered better. His heresy was followed that night by a fearful thunderstorm, during which a thunderbolt hurtled into the royal chamber. The storm only abated its fury when the wise king admitted his error.

The squat strength of the castle at Coca in Old Castile presents a very different appearance from the picturesque towers and canopies of the Alcazar at Segovia. The castle is built of brick, and its style clearly reflects the enduring influence of the Moorish elements in Spanish culture. The castle is roughly square, consisting of two curtain walls around a central courtyard; both walls are heavily fortified with turrets and towers, while the outer one is also protected by a steep batter, which rises halfway up its height. The corners of the outer battlements are also defended by projecting polygonal towers, which are further strengthened by clustering turrets; these are connected by a wall-walk running the length of the fortifications and equipped with a series of machicolations. The reed-like treatment of the brickwork on the battlements is a characteristic of Castel Coca, but although it is the most obvious feature of the external decoration, it is by no means the only one. On every part of the structure there are decorative motifs that lighten the stern appearance of the fortifications; the most interesting examples are perhaps found on the pointed bases of the projecting turrets. These are embellished with chevron and herring-bone patterns, either painted on or formed by the layout of the bricks themselves. But despite its decoration, the fortress of Coca is unmistakably built on military lines; perhaps the strongest expression of this is in the square Tower of Homage in the north of the inner enceinte, which was built during the 15th century and reconstructed and extended during the 18th. The oldest part of the

This fine view of the Alcazar at Segovia dramatically illustrates the castle's dominating position over the surrounding countryside.

structure (and one of the most formidable) is found in the mighty lower courses of the wall on the south side of the outer enceinte.

Another largely brick-built fortress of Old Castile is the Castillo de la Mota at Medina. As the name implies, it stands on a low hill, or *mote*; it was built for King John II in the mid-15th century and was one of the court residences of Castile. Queen Isabella died here in 1504, and over the drawbridge gate are carved the arms of the two Catholic monarchs, Ferdinand and Isabella. The castle consists of four main sections: the outer barbican, which encloses the parade ground or Plaza de las Armas; the great brick curtain wall with its battlements and round turrets; the castle proper within this; and the lofty Homage Tower, again with corner turrets and also with battlements rising above the machicolations.

Last of the splendid fortresses of Old Castile to be considered in this chapter is the castle of Peñafiel in the modern province of Valladolid. Standing on a low hill, which falls sharply away from its walls, it seems to sail like an iron-clad battleship with a pointed prow cutting the clear, sunlit air. Square amidships is the solid bulk of the Homage Tower, a more stalwart version of the Tower of John II at Segovia, and a further example of a rectangular keep with round, hanging turrets and prominent machicolations. The original building on the site was built in the 11th century, but the ramparts of the present castle were begun in the early 1300s and the keep dates from the 15th century. Both the simplicity and strength of the structure and the workmanlike choice of the site clearly express the straight-forward military purpose of this castle, which, like so many of Castilian fortresses, was once a mighty stronghold for defending fields and villages from Christian neighbours or Moorish enemies.

A second view of Peñafiel showing the steep slope of the hill as it falls away from the fortress.

CHAPTER 9

CASTEL DEL MONTE

Castel del Monte stands like a crown on the summit of a gentle hill, looking eastward towards the blue shores of the Adriatic and dominating the surrounding desolate landscape of the Murge of Apuleia in southern Italy. Built from the golden limestone of the district, it is the most beautiful and probably the most famous of the many castles designed by Frederick II, Emperor of the West and King of Sicily, for his relaxation and diversion. But its peaceful aspect should not be overemphasised. In its present state, it is perfectly defensible. (It was used as a prison by Frederick's successor Charles of Anjou.) Furthermore, there are signs that the main entrance was originally protected by a portcullis, and it is possible that the present castle was intended as a central keep within a curtain wall. A contemporary chronicler said of Frederick, 'he built palaces of great beauty and size with a passionate enthusiasm, as if he would live for ever, though in fact he inhabited none of them; he had castles and towers erected in towns and on mountain peaks as one who lived in daily fear of attack. But his real aim was to demonstrate to the world his great power and to instil into men fear and admiration for him, and to impress the glory of his name so deeply on their memories that it should never be obliterated by the oblivion of time.'

Many of the castles referred to by the chronicler still survive, among them the Castel Ursino in Catania, Sicily, and the castles of Bari and Trani. These belong to the series of military works that Frederick began after his return south from his German territories in the 1220s. The kingdom of Sicily had gone through an extremely turbulent period in the thirty years that followed the death of his predecessor, William II, the last of the Norman kings. In 1220, therefore, Frederick issued an edict ordering the demolition of all

Part of the walls of the Castel Ursino built by Frederick II in Catania, Sicily. By the second quarter of the 13th century the round tower had almost displaced the rectangular tower in major fortresses but, as can be seen from a comparison of this picture with the view of Bari on p. 152, the emperor's architects also used the older technique of rectangular towers. 149

non-royal castles built during this time. This policy of destruction and the construction of his own series of fortresses intended to restore the supremacy of his royal authority beyond any possible shadow of doubt.

There are indications that the emperor took a direct personal interest in the design of many of his castles, and it seems probable that he was himself the chief architect of Castel del Monte. But although some scholars are now prepared to accept the emperor as architect, it is interesting to note that as late as the 19th century, local tradition had a different story to tell about the castle's origins. Edward Lear, in his *Journals of a Landscape Painter in Southern Calabria* (1850), records the tale told him by his guide on the long ride back from Castel del Monte to the town where he was staying. It was believed that, far from having designed the castle, Frederick had not even visited the site. So, eager for news of the building's progress, he sent a young courtier to investigate and report. The young gallant, however, was delayed at Malfi by the charms of some local beauty. When a messenger arrived ordering his immediate return to the imperial court at Naples, the courtier, not daring to waste any more time in actually inspecting the new castle, decided to bluff it out. He reported to the emperor that the work was completely unsatisfactory. Angrily Frederick sent a peremptory letter to the architect, telling him to consider himself in disgrace and asking him to explain himself at the capital. The terrified man begged to be allowed to say farewell to his family, and, in one of the rooms of the now almost completed building, killed his wife and children and then committed suicide. When the news reached the court, Frederick decided to investigate for himself. We continue in the words of Lear: 'What was Frederick's indignation at beholding one of the most beautiful buildings doomed, through the falseness of his messenger, to remain incomplete and polluted by the blood of his most skilful subject and his innocent family. Foaming with rage, he dragged the offender by the hair of his head to the top of the highest tower, and with his own hands threw him down as a sacrifice to the memory of the architect and his family so cruelly and wantonly destroyed.'

Whoever may have been the architect—and it seems in fact reasonable to assume that Frederick did have a hand in the design—Castel del Monte was a notable landmark in the architectural history of southern Italy. When it was built, the Gothic style (conveniently dated from the work of the Abbé Suger at St Denis in the 1130s) had been evolving in France for over a century. Outside France, its

Opposite, the honey-coloured stone and domestic scale of Castel del Monte are deceptive. This castle, like the others described in this book, would have been quite defensible.

Below, Frederick II's castle at Trani off the Adriatic coast of Apulia was built in 1233–49. The port was exposed to the depredations of Arab corsairs and fortresses of this kind played an essential part in the protection of the townships and ports.

development was slower and its adoption far from universal. In southern Italy, it was virtually unknown; it was in fact Frederick and his architects who introduced a basic Gothic principle—the ribbed vault—to the area. Possibly he was influenced by his travels in his German territories, where new cathedrals, heavily influenced by French originals, were springing up. Yet although basically Gothic in conception, Castel del Monte also includes several classical elements, while the luxury of the living quarters betrays the influence both of the Arab East and Byzantium. This diversity is the keynote to the castle's design as it was to the social life of the court of Frederick II.

At the entrance of the building, the visitor is immediately confronted with the rival claims of the Gothic and classical styles. The doorway is flanked by pilasters with Corinthian capitals surmounted by a pediment; according to records, immediately over the door there was originally a bust of the emperor, crowned with a halo of the sun's rays in the style of Roman imperial portraiture. Yet above this obviously classical composition is a mullioned window that is purely Gothic in concept. More examples of the classicising influence of

Right, the main entrance to Castel del Monte, which vividly shows the slowly reviving interest in classical architectural motifs combined with a lingering Gothicism: the classical order of the gateway itself contrasts with the pointed arch and mullioned window.

Below, the castle at Bari, another of the numerous fortresses and palaces built during the reign of Frederick II. Note the pronounced batter on the corner bastion of the outer wall.

Above, a view of Castel del Monte that clearly illustrates the origin of the fortress's nickname of 'the Crown of Apulia'. The castle has a less obviously military character than the other three castles illustrated, but recently scholars have come to believe that it was intended to be a defensive point as well as a hunting lodge.

153

south Italian architecture are found in the remarkably handsome first-floor windows of the inner courtyard. These originally opened out like french windows on to a balcony running round the courtyard, allowing the courtiers and their ladies to sun themselves in the shelter of the circling walls. Bas-reliefs were carved in the walls beneath the balcony and one of them survives; it depicts a horseman, naked except for a short Greek cloak clasped at the neck.

Apart from these reliefs, the castle was decorated with numerous other sculptures and carvings, such as the head with ass's ears in one of the main ground-floor rooms and the head of Bacchus in the roof of another. As well as these works by contemporary artists, Frederick embellished his little castle with the classical sculptures of which he was a keen collector. An even clearer indication of his love of ancient art was the triumphal arch at Capua, which again seems to have been designed by the emperor himself. This fine work, pulled down by the Spanish authorities in 1557, was decorated with bas-reliefs and busts of the emperor and his ministers; it was even thought by later generations to have been genuinely Roman and merely renovated by Frederick. Surviving fragments and Renaissance drawings have enabled scholars to build up a picture of the gate in its original state. In his short monograph on the subject, Creswell Shearer points out that not only the architectural design but also the sculptures themselves are more in tune with the classical rather than the Gothic spirit. The proportions closely follow those of the human body whereas sculptures in northern Europe tended to distort them to give a vertical emphasis.

The octagonal plan of the building already mentioned was repeated in the design of the towers, which originally rose some six feet above the level of the walls. The main living rooms were situated between the inner and outer walls while the servants' quarters, storage space and so on were accommodated in the corner towers. The domestic luxury of the whole establishment was remarkable by European standards of the time, and had more in common perhaps with the castles and palaces of the Franks of Outremer than with those of Europe. Because of their position between the two octagonal walls, the main rooms are trapezoid in shape; there are sixteen rooms in all, eight on the ground floor and eight on the first floor. Compared with other royal apartments of the time, they are small—about 35 feet by 22 feet. (For this reason, it seems, Castel del Monte was demoted to use as a prison by the French conqueror of Sicily, Charles of Anjou.) But whatever the rooms lack in size they made up

in luxury. The plumbing was remarkably advanced; many of the rooms had baths and latrines supplied by water cisterns in the roof. Though traces of an inlaid marble floor can be seen in one of the ground-floor rooms, the actual furnishings have long since disappeared. From our knowledge of Frederick's taste, however, we can assume that Persian and other Eastern rugs and carpets would have covered the floors of the main apartments and that in the emperor's own rooms volumes from his large collection of books would have been a prominent feature.

The builder of Castel del Monte was a man of varied tastes and talents. To his contemporaries he was a controversial figure, who was variously known as *stupor mundi* (wonder of the world) and the antichrist; for posterity his fame has been kept alive not only by his castles, as he hoped, but by the stories associated with his name,

Originally a balcony would have run around the interior of the courtyard and the photograph, opposite, shows one of the doorways leading from the inner rooms on to this balcony.

When in use, the rooms of the castle-palace would have presented a splendid and rich appearance, hung with rich tapestries and with Arab and Oriental carpets on the floors. Above left, a view of marble pillars and a doorway that still retains some of its marble facing. Note the capitals of the pillars, which are typical of Gothic architecture throughout Europe.

Above, a close-up of the main gate showing the surviving sculptured lion perched on the capital of a strange variant of a Corinthian column. 155

Above, some of the elegant rib vaulting at Castel del Monte—another indication of the way in which Frederick II's architects introduced principles of Gothic structure not generally known in southern Italy at this period. Note the decorative boss at the junction of the vaults.

Left, another interior, this time showing one of the castle's splendid and elaborate fireplaces. The room is lit from one of the large windows in the outer walls, shown on the opposite page.

Right, part of the so-called Throne Room on the first floor, which exhibits to the full the splendid lines and spacious treatment of the castle interior. Here again the marble pillars are still in place and the splendid window is framed with a marble arch.

157

which stand out from the conventional (though erroneous) picture of medieval Europe as a society of religious conformity and intellectual stagnation.

Frederick of Hohenstaufen was the son of Constance of Sicily and Henry VI, the Holy Roman Emperor. He was able to establish his claim to both these inheritances, and thus the papacy found itself encircled by territory belonging to its long-standing enemy, the emperor. Frederick's attempts to unite his two realms were fiercely opposed by Pope Innocent IV and his successors. This confrontation between the spiritual father of Christendom and its most powerful temporal ruler (who was excommunicated three times) broke for ever the might of the Holy Roman Empire and greatly weakened the authority of the papacy.

Although bitter and lengthy, this was by no means the first clash between the spiritual and temporal powers of medieval Europe, though the personality of Frederick and the life of his southern court that so shocked and amazed his contemporaries introduced a new element to the struggle. His menagerie of wild beasts, the Oriental dress and manners of his court were piquant experiences for the average European, while his patronage of both Christian and Moslem scholars and the laxity of his private life (he is even said to have kept a harem) were utterly scandalising. Typical of Frederick's disregard for convention was his crusade of 1227 (undertaken while he was still under the papal ban of excommunication), which ended not in victory but in a treaty with the sultan, who matched Frederick in intellectual curiosity and was equally suspect to his co-religionists. After his coronation as King of Jerusalem in the Holy City, where he visited Moslem mosques, Frederick returned to Europe. Whether or not, as has been suggested, the design of Castel del Monte was influenced by Frederick's experiences both in the East and in Germany, it is certain that his cosmopolitan court was of deep significance in the history of European culture. The mingling of Provençal poets, German minnesingers and Moslem and southern Italian poets produced a Sicilian court style that affected the *dolce stil nuovo* of the 13th-century poets of northern Italy. The emperor's passion for classical art, fostered by his view of himself as the descendant of the Caesars, led to work such as that of the gate at Capua or the Castel del Monte, which in turn influenced the sculptor and architect Andrea Pisano. In this little castle in Apulia are concentrated the wide-ranging taste of its builder and the influence of his reign on

European culture.

CHAPTER 10

CHATEAU DE CHILLON

The Château of Chillon, once the residence of the counts of Savoy and now the proudest monument in the Swiss canton of Vaud, stands on an island site by the shores of Lake Geneva near to the town of Montreux. It has the romantic appearance of all castles in a water setting and also their natural strength, for it is not only provided with a ready-made moat but is also built on solid rock. The cluster of walls and tiled roofs we see today—highly picturesque yet at the same time extremely strong—was mainly the product of building operations most of which took place during a period of about four centuries, though the early history of the castle is somewhat obscure.

The first castle on the site (dating from the 10th century) comprised the main donjon in the centre of the island and a curtain wall that roughly followed the inner boundary of the present courtyard. The tower, known as the Tower of Alinge (which was about a storey lower than it is today), was one of the many battlemented stone towers that sprang up all over Europe at that time. The origin of the name is lost in the mists of the past, but it may have been called after the founder's family or possibly, as occasionally happened, after the builder himself.

Further building took place in the early 11th century when an outer line of fortifications following the edge of the island and the tower on the northern tip (now known as the Tower of the Dukes) were added. From the time it was built until the castle ceased to be a nobleman's residence, this tower was the centre of the living quarters used by the counts and dukes who lived there; the other halls and rooms were grouped around it between the inner and outer curtain walls built around the north end of the island. The next building phase took place two centuries later, when the castle at Chillon

Above, the Château at Chillon from the lake. The lower windows are, for reasons of defence, mere arrow slits. Above them, on the left, can be seen the windows of the Great Hall, the Hall of the Knights on the first floor, and to the right, the windows of the châtelaine's room.

Left, a view from the hillside above clearly showing the layout of the castle. To the left, the square tower guarding the outer courtyard and the entrance, in the centre the Tower of Alinge, and to the right, the Tower of the Dukes.

(despite many minor later additions and improvements by successive counts, dukes and governors) acquired the main features of its present-day form. This extensive work was carried out for Peter II, Count of Savoy from 1263 to 1268 and master of Chillon for several years before his accession.

The territories of Savoy, which straddled the modern boundaries between France and Italy and included part of modern Switzerland, had a long and varied history that was inextricably linked to the fortunes of its ruling house. It belonged—like the county of Flanders in the north, whose counts established themselves in the castle at Ghent—to that no-man's-land between two great European powers, the kingdom of France and the Holy Roman Empire. When the empire of Charlemagne was first divided at the Treaty of Verdun in 843, Savoy was one of the territories assigned to the Emperor Lothair I, but soon afterwards it was engrossed by the kingdom of Burgundy and later still by the kingdom of Arles. It became an independent territory during the 11th century, when it was seized by an ambitious nobleman of the kingdom of Arles, Humbert Whitehands, whose successors extended their territories to take in large tracts of land surrounding French Savoy and Piedmont, including the lands around Chillon.

In the 13th century, Peter II of Savoy chose Chillon as his favourite residence. He was related by the marriage of his nieces Eleanor and Beatrice of Provence to King Henry III of England and Charles of Anjou—two of the most powerful rulers in Europe. And like many of his relations, he took advantage of King Henry's generosity to his wife's family to carve out a career for himself in England. He became an intimate adviser to the king and played a considerable part in the plots and intrigues of the baronial wars that centred around Henry and Simon de Montfort. Indeed one of the barons' grievances was the number of foreign advisers at Henry's court and the honours that he bestowed on them. Peter's younger brother, Boniface, was given the archbishopric of Canterbury, while Peter himself became Earl of Richmond and was presented with a palace in the Strand on the site of the present Savoy Hotel. Apart from the survival of this name, the association between the house of Plantagenet and the house of Savoy bore more practical fruits during the reign of Henry's son, Edward I, in the person of James St George. As we have already seen, this Savoyard architect had done a great deal of work for the counts of Savoy before he came to England in the service of the English king to supervise the building of the great Welsh fortresses.

The castle at Chillon stands on its rocky island separated from the mainland by some thirty feet of water. As has already been pointed out, it is a naturally strong site; it is also strategically well placed for controlling routes to the Great St Bernard Pass over the Alps into Italy. On the land side, as well as the natural obstacle of the moat, the castle is defended by a double line of walls—the outer strengthened by three towers, the inner by a glacis, or plinth, which slopes down through the line of the second wall to the water's edge. It resembles the vast defensive works round the southern redoubt of Krak des Chevaliers, which was built about 150 years later.

The castle is approached by an 18th-century bridge, which replaced the original drawbridge; to the south of the bridge was a dock—a necessary part of any fortress on a natural stretch of water. The visitor passes through the gatehouse into the outer courtyard and from there through a second gateway leading to the inner courtyard; this is divided in effect into two wards by the great donjon. Spanning this division along the lakeside is a long building housing the castle kitchen and the two great halls. To the north of this are the main ducal apartments, of which the great *camera domini*—the duke's chamber—occupying the first floor of the Tower of the Dukes is by far the most important. Although the capital of the duchy was established at Chambéry during the 13th century, Chillon continued to be used at frequent intervals by the counts and dukes, and the *camera domini* (which, like the other ducal apartments, was closed when the ruler was not in residence) was embellished by successive generations of the house of Savoy and remained the main chamber of the castle after it had been taken over by the city of Berne in the 16th century. On the walls are traces of three distinct sets of paintings of which the finest were those commissioned in 1341 by Count Aymon. They were painted in tempera by Jean de Grandson and George of Florence, and seem to have been intended as imitations of the tapestry hangings that were the usual form of wall decoration. The subjects depicted—animals and legendary scenes—were typical of the genre. Over the fireplace was an equestrian figure impaling a monster on his lance—presumably St George and the Dragon—while around the walls are animals, natural and fabulous, in a wooden landscape. As well as a bull and a lion (which were still found in parts of Europe) were camel, antelope and leopard as well as a griffin and a dragon. The red ceiling is decorated with white crosses; other decorations dating from the 13th century are mostly geometrical designs—alternate red and green horizontal bandings and red and white

162

Above, a view looking towards the gatehouse between the inner and outer curtain walls on the land side. Note the glacis descending from the inner wall.

Right, the natural moat formed by a creek of the lake between the island and the bank. Once, wooden beams, like those jutting from the towers, would have carried a brattice when the castle was under siege.

checker patterns. On the ceilings, green rafters are divided by white plaster areas embellished with red cinquefoils, stars and arabesques. Next to this room on the west side is a small chamber reserved exclusively for the counts and dukes.

From this little room another door leads into the armorial hall, now called the Hall of the Knights, from whose windows there is a superb view of the Lake of Geneva stretching away to the west. On the floor below is the main public chamber of the castle, the Great Hall itself. It was here that ceremonial banquets would have been held, that the counts and dukes would have received their vassals and dispensed justice to their subjects. The two halls were built in the time of Count Peter II, but were considerably altered during the centuries that followed his reign. The magnificent vaults below them,

The Château seen from the land to the south, opposite, even now provides a formidable as well as a decorative sight. The original dock would have been on the near side of the bridge in the foreground.

Below, the inner courtyard showing the Tower of the Dukes, and, on the left, a window of the Great Hall.

Top left, the Hall of the Knights, the upper of the two halls overlooking the lake. With its checkered wall pattern and decorated ceiling, it gives a fair impression of the style of 13th-century interior decoration.

Centre left, the Great Hall of the castle looking southwards. Note the handsome panelled ceiling.

Below left, the room of the châtelaine overlooking the lake and the outer courtyard. There are still traces of the 13th-century chevron pattern wall paintings over the fireplace. From the late 14th century, tapestries became the more usual form of wall decoration.

Below, the camera domini in the Tower of the Dukes; although very faded, the general design of the wall paintings can still be made out.

however, are more or less as they were when completed in the 13th century, and are among the finest to be found in the castles of medieval Europe. (An obvious comparison can be made between them and the great subterranean stables at Ghent, and it is perhaps not too fanciful to suggest that they were originally intended for the same purpose.) The rockface has been hewn out to form a long chamber with windows overlooking the surface of the lake; the roof and superstructure above is carried on vaults springing from corbels on the wall and the rockface and supported down the centre on eight pillars. Whatever function this magnificent structure originally fulfilled, it was, like the basement stables at Ghent, used by later generations as a prison. The miserable wretches confined in this dank and terrible dungeon, who were chained to rings let into the pillars and the rock, include perhaps the most famous prisoner in the whole of European history. His name was François Bonivard—the Prisoner of Chillon of Byron's famous poem, which was inspired by the poet's visit to the castle in 1816.

As so often happens, the romantic hero of this poem was very different from the man himself. Byron's brave enemy of tyranny, who was born about 1493, was a cleric of dubious morals and fiery temperament. His first defiant gestures against Duke Charles III of Savoy—specifically, his support of the citizens of Geneva in their struggle to throw off ducal authority—seem to have been prompted by his anger at the duke's encroachment on the privileges of his own abbey of St Victor at Geneva. He was imprisoned by the duke for three years, between 1519 and 1521, and again in 1530 for another six years in the castle of Chillon. The first two years of his confinement were not too unpleasant, but he was then transferred to the vaulted cellar—possibly on the specific orders of the duke—which he later pronounced, somewhat exaggeratedly, to be below the level of the lake. The pillar to which he was chained has been variously identified; Byron put his money and indeed his name on the third one from the door. Bonivard himself claimed to have worn a path in the rock floor by his incessant pacing up and down, so we can assume he was not perpetually tethered. Yet in spite of Bonivard's questionable standing as a champion of freedom and the probably exaggerated hardships of his imprisonment, the day of his release by the victorious troops of Berne must have been a very happy one. Geneva hailed him as a hero, made him an honorary citizen and commissioned him to write a history of the town (which was not in fact published until the 19th century).

The vaulted cellar beneath the Great Hall; the second pillar from the right is thought to be the one to which Bonivard was chained.

Throughout the middle ages, Geneva struggled to assert its independence against its bishop—a goal that seemed even more difficult to achieve as the 15th century advanced and the dukes of Savoy gained increasing control of the bishopric. During the 1510s the bishop and the duke joined in the suppression of the hard-won liberties of the town, but Geneva's alliance with the powerful city of Berne forced the bishop to flee in 1527. But he returned nine years later and laid siege to the city. The siege was raised and Geneva liberated by its Bernese allies; and as the result of their victorious campaign, the castle of Chillon, for so long the proud residence of the dukes of Savoy, was brought under the control of the mighty city-state of Berne.

A panorama that reveals the full splendour of Chillon in its rugged alpine setting.

CHAPTER 11

THE WARTBURG

The Wartburg, formerly the castle of the Landgraves of Thuringia, perches on a lofty outcrop of rock to the south-west of the little German town of Eisenach. When viewed from the wooded valleys below, the rock appears formidable, yet the castle itself, clustering on the summit, looks at first sight like a village, with a manor-house, church towers and half-timbered houses. In fact, the manor-house is the great house of the landgraves, the church towers are the two fortified belfries and the half-timbered houses are the coverings to the wall-walks, from which the defenders used to fire down on their besiegers below.

According to legend, the castle was established in 1067 by Ludwig the Leaper, the first of the house of Ludowinger. Out hunting one day, Ludwig and his companions came across the mysterious mountain of the Wartburg. The count decided to take possession of it as a site for a new castle, but the local inhabitants contested his claim. The wily Ludwig thereupon returned to the Wartburg with a large supply of earth, which he scattered over the summit of the mountain, declaring that the land now belonged to him. His twelve companions stuck their swords in the ground and swore to uphold the count's claim—an oath they repeated before the emperor. Count Ludwig thereupon began to build his new castle within the ring formed by the twelve swords; it was said that the spirits of the twelve wicked barons could be seen hovering like will-o'-the-wisps over the hilts of their dishonoured weapons. In 1130 the Holy Roman Emperor Lothair raised the house of Ludowinger to the position of landgraves (or princes); and during the reign of Ludwig III (1172–90), the family acquired the territories of Thuringia, Hesse and the Palatinate and a corresponding measure of power. The prestige of the Ludowinger and

A view of the Wartburg from the south, showing the South Tower and the landgrave's house, which reveals the strength of the site; in the middle ages the trees would have been cleared to leave no cover for attackers. 169

The west front of the landgrave's house from the north-west. This photograph, taken after the restoration of the late 1950s, gives an idea of the splendour of the Romanesque arcades and clearly shows the slope on which the Great Hall was built.

their influence in German affairs were further increased by the fact that Ludwig was a cousin of the great Emperor Frederick I Barbarossa. Not surprisingly then, it was during this reign that the first buildings on any scale were constructed on the Wartburg. The landgrave's house, one of the finest examples of Romanesque domestic architecture in Europe, was also begun at this time and completed under Ludwig's brother and successor, Hermann I.

The castle on the Wartburg was built by a rising family of petty nobles as their chief residence and as an expression of their growing power. For later generations, it was to become a symbol of a legendary past, whose glorious achievements served as an inspiration for the new, unified Germany of the future. Later still, the romantic idealisation of the middle ages during the 19th century intensified the respect in which the Wartburg was held. Yet by 1817 a great deal of the castle's original structure was either obscured by later additions or in a state of dilapidation; the central belfry had entirely disappeared. As a result, a long-term programme of extensive rebuilding and restoration was carried out from 1838 to 1891. Because the work inevitably expressed the romantic preoccupations of the period, the architects were sometimes more concerned with dramatic effect than with historical accuracy. New mosaics and furnishings were designed for the living rooms, and paintings depicting high points of the castle's history were commissioned from the romantic painter

170

Left, a view of the gatehouse with its draw-bridge, the wall-walk covered in with half-timbered hoarding and, in the background, the reconstructed belfry. On the extreme left can be seen the end of the landgrave's house.

Below, the first courtyard looking down towards the gatehouse with the wall-walk on the right and the Vogtei on the left. It was in this part of the castle that Luther stayed during 1521–2.

171

Moritz von Schwind. The paintings have survived, but much of the architectural work has been remodelled during the massive reconstruction, sponsored by the East German authorities, that took place under the supervision of Dr Siegfried Asche in 1957–60.

From the east, the castle's most prominent features are the landgrave's house with its arcaded windows; the two towers behind it to the north and south; and stretching northwards, the wall surmounted by the half-timbered penthouse covering the wall-walks. The gatehouse formed the northernmost point of the enceinte and is approached by a drawbridge. Passing through it, the visitor finds himself in a courtyard with the Ritterhaus and Vogtei to his right and, in front of him, the building known as the Dirnitz. Although heavily restored during the 19th century, the Ritterhaus, or knight's house, is one of the oldest parts of the castle, and may have been the landgrave's residence until the 1220s. Next to it stands the Vogtei (again a basically medieval structure), which, as is reflected in its German name, came to be used as the residence of the town governor of Eisenach. In the centre of the castle complex is the belfry (German, *Berchfrit*), the main defensive work. It was severely damaged by lightning in about 1317, had become structurally unsound by the 16th century and by the late 18th century had totally collapsed. The present structure is a complete reconstruction dating from 1853–59 and exemplifies the dubious accuracy of much of the work done at that time. Each side of the building (which is square) is in fact some five feet shorter than those of the original; and although the earlier foundations were unearthed as the reconstruction was in progress, the tower was completed without reference to the original. During the late 1950s, the foundations of the first tower were again uncovered and these, with the foundations of an earlier hall, are now open to inspection.

At the end of the courtyard (formed by the Dirnitz, the landgrave's house and the curtain wall) stands the South Tower, the oldest part of the whole surviving structure. Possibly the first tower on this site was made of wood, but the existing building in stone dates from the late 12th or early 13th century and has an entrance above ground level—a characteristic feature of early keeps. The door was approached by an external wooden staircase that could, in case of emergency, be knocked away. To the east of the courtyard is the landgrave's house, the most impressive of all the buildings at the Wartburg. Most of the recent restoration has been concentrated on this building, which as it now stands can be accepted as an accurate representation

172

Above, the interior of the restored Rittersaal or Knight's Chamber on the ground floor of the landgrave's house. The massive arches of the vaultings are effectively relieved by the sinuous and grotesque eagle figures of the carved capital.

Above right, the restored interior of the Sängersaal or Hall of the Singers. Note the timber-beamed ceiling supporting the two central pillars with carved foliage capitals. The painting is one of many romantic reconstructions of the poetic contest, known as the Wartburgkrieg, by the 19th-century artist Moritz von Schwind.

Far right, the interior of the ground-floor arcade of the landgrave's house. This part of the castle was built in the late 12th century, but was altered in the 17th; it was only restored to its original state in 1956.

of the medieval original. For this reason, it is worth looking at in some detail.

Because it is built on a slope, the main three-storeyed structure is supported at the south end on two undercrofts, which, with the first two storeys, were built during the reign of Ludwig III. The lower of the first two storeys (which originally included a hall at the northern end, behind the belfry) comprise two square vaulted rooms converging on a central pillar. The more northerly room is now known as the Rittersaal, or knight's chamber. The next floor also consists of two rooms, roofed with wooden beams and rafters supported by two pillars. The northern room, the Sängersaal (hall of the singers) is traditionally believed to be the scene of the Wartburgkrieg (which is described later in the chapter). In the original building the second floor was one large room; this was divided off to form a chapel at the beginning of the 14th century. On both floors, there is a gallery running the full length of the building and lit by the superb arcades that are such a notable feature of the courtyard façade. The great banqueting hall, which makes up the third storey, was added under Landgrave Hermann, and forms a satisfying crown to the whole building. Here too the arcades run the full length of the room, and again the windows overlooking the outer wall of the fortress are more widely spaced for reasons of defence. The three floors of the building are linked by an internal staircase.

Today's visitor to the Wartburg can also see an interesting collection of works of art, costume, furniture and armour as well as the carvings and paintings that decorate the castle itself. An early 14th-century wall painting of the Apostles survives in the chapel while the capitals of the pillars offer an intriguing display of medieval figure carving. Many of the motifs, such as the griffin heads and the palmettes (fan-shapes), are typical of medieval architecture in general; others—such as the pecking eagles, the angels' and demons' heads and the lions—are more localised, and are similar to carvings in churches at Naumburg, Freiburg and other neighbouring towns.

The veneration felt for the Wartburg during the 19th century was based on various episodes in the castle's history that took place during the reign of Hermann at the landgrave's house itself. Hermann had visited France as a young man and there absorbed the ideas of the school of courtly love—the idealisation of romance and chivalry that was to play such an important part in medieval culture. On his return to Germany, his court became the meeting place for German poets of the new school—the minnesingers. The brilliance of Hermann's court was commemorated in a poem written in the second half of the 13th century, the *Wartburgkrieg* (the Battle of the Wartburg). The writer of this poem describes a poetic contest (a convention of the school) between two representatives of rival patrons —a contest that was supposedly held before Landgrave Hermann at the castle in 1206–7. In the first part of the poem, Heinrich von Ofterdingen catalogues the superior merits of his patron compared with those of the king of France (championed by Walther von der Vogelweide) and the landgrave himself (championed by Wolfram von Eschenbach). Not surprisingly, Wolfram and his supporters are victorious, and Heinrich is lucky to escape the penalty of death prescribed for the loser. The actual contest described in the poem is almost certainly fictitious, but it gives some idea of the kind of gatherings that must have often taken place in the Sängersaal.

Hermann was succeeded by his son Ludwig, whose wife, Elisabeth of Hungary, was to be the centre of another—and rather different— story in the castle's history. She was brought to Thuringia as a child of four and brought up in the castle. From this early age, her generosity to the common people aroused comment in a rigidly class-conscious society. As she grew older, her reputation for saintliness increased. After the death of her husband in the crusades in 1227, she left the castle, renounced her former life and even her family and devoted herself to the poor and sick. Four years after her death, she

was canonised and a church was dedicated to her at Marburg. Her story was also commemorated by Franz von Liszt in an oratorio that he conducted at a performance in the banqueting hall of the landgrave's house in 1867.

Perhaps the most famous person associated with the castle is Martin Luther, who stayed there between 1521 and 1522. After his refusal to recant at the Diet of Worms in April 1521, Luther was on the run both from the Church and from the Emperor Charles V. Perhaps the danger was less great than it appeared, but nevertheless he took refuge for twelve months in the castle of the Elector of Saxony on the Wartburg. The episode has a cloak-and-dagger quality with all the characters trying to keep Luther's movements secret. From Worms, Luther went to Eisenach and then to the little township of Mohra, where he spent the night. On the morning of May 4, he set out by coach towards the south, but was waylaid by highwaymen in the neighbourhood of the Wartburg. The coach driver, who was allowed to go free, drove back to report that the great man had been taken. Meanwhile Luther himself was escorted by his captors to the fortress on the orders of his friend the castellan, Hans von Berlesch.

Once in the castle, Luther was kept out of sight for several weeks. He then appeared with the fashionably cut beard, clothes and sword of a knight, calling himself Junker Jörg (Knight George). It is hard to believe that the disguise can have been very effective; Luther must

Above left, Luther's room in the Vogtei after its restoration in the 1950s. Here he wrote his great translation of the New Testament. During his stay, he was disguised as a member of the landed gentry; the engraving of him by his friend Cranach, above, can be seen over the fireplace.

One of the most fascinating features of the Wartburg is the carving of the Romanesque capitals of the pillars. The two capitals, opposite, in the landgrave's room, depicting lions and birds (apparently falcons) are typical of the beautiful architectural detailing at the Wartburg. 175

have made a peculiar knight. He spent most of his time in the little room reserved for him in the Vogtei and, when he did emerge, voiced opinions very different from those of the landed gentry; the junker was once heard to remark that hunting was a suitable occupation for people who had nothing better to do. During his time at the Wartburg, Luther wrote a series of pamphlets violently critical of his theological rivals, and made a German translation of the New Testament. This task occupied about two months of his exile in his 'island of Patmos', so the Wartburg became the birthplace of one of the great landmarks of the German Reformation.

With the three-hundredth anniversary of that Reformation, the Wartburg was once again the focus of German national conscience. On October 18, 1817 a long procession of students wound up the slopes of the hill on which the castle stands and assembled in the historic hall of the landgrave's house. They had gathered to commemorate not only Luther's defiance of the Church of Rome but also the German wars of liberation against Napoleon, and speeches at the Wartburg recalled these great moments in the history of Germany and called passionately for the unification of the petty German states into one great nation. Thus the castle of the landgraves came to be a symbol of a new Germany in which the successors of the landgraves would have no place.

Left, an engraving depicting the procession of students approaching the Wartburg to attend celebrations commemorating the Reformation.

Opposite, the lofty peak on which the Wartburg was built—an ideal site for a stronghold.

176

CHAPTER 12

'S GRAVENSTEEN GHENT

The Gravensteen, the castle of the Counts of Flanders, stands in a wide moat near the centre of the modern town of Ghent. Yet the first castle (which was probably built in the ninth century) would have been outside the township. Later, the counts and the burghers of Ghent were to engage in a long battle for control over the city. This fight was eventually won by the townsmen; the merchants, whose corn exchange on the Graselei was built within a generation of the new castle, outlasted the counts, and today the fortress is surrounded on all sides by their spacious houses and churches.

The struggle for independence is the focal point of the history of both the castle and the town until the mid-14th century, when the counts moved to another residence, the Prinzenhof. From then on, the Gravensteen was used more and more for ceremonial occasions; parts of it were converted into government offices and even, for a time in the 19th century, into a factory. This decline is paralleled in the history of many other great castles, but in one respect the Gravensteen was luckier than some: in the 1880s it was thoroughly restored under the direction of the Ghent architect J. de Waele. The restorers' aim was a faithful reconstruction of the original design, and we can feel fairly confident that the overall appearance of the castle today is much as it was during the 13th century.

By the beginning of the 10th century the counts had erected a moated stone castle, which forms the lower level of the present keep. At this time, the counts seem to have been well established, but in the early 12th century, the citizens of Ghent gave a foretaste of their future independence and opposed the succession of the new count, William of Cliton, in favour of their own candidate, Thierry of Alsace. With their support, Thierry won his claim, yet by the end of

178

the century his successor, Philip, found the prosperous citizenry once more encroaching on his authority. He therefore rebuilt and extended the castle 'to humble the overbearing arrogance of the men of Ghent, proud of their wealth and building for themselves houses fortified like towers', to quote the contemporary chronicler, Giselebert of Mons. In 1179, the year before the count began his new fortress, the Archbishop of Rheims denounced the Ghent merchants in similar terms: 'Fortune has smiled on the citizens. They have acquired great riches and built themselves great houses and in their haughty pride usurp the jurisdictions and domains of the count.' It seems then that the castle was primarily intended to demonstrate the count's superior strength; it was certainly a remarkable demonstration.

Below left, part of the wall-walk and interior of two of the hanging turrets overlooking the moat at the Gravensteen. When the castle was prepared for war a platform, supported by wooden beams, would have been set up at 'first-floor' level. From this archers would fire through the embrasures of the battlements.

Below, a view from the keep of the castle of the Counts overlooking the town of Ghent epitomises the confrontation of the military stronghold of the aristocratic family with the houses and great churches of the prosperous trading city.

It has been suggested that the castle's design was influenced by the count's experience of the fortifications in the Levant during the crusades. The hanging turrets of the enceinte, which give the castle its extremely individual appearance, have no exact parallel among crusader castles; but the tactical ideas behind them—that of projecting towers from which firepower could be directed to protect the curtain wall—may well have been evolved by the military architects of Byzantium. None of the turrets at Ghent (except the watch tower across the yard from the entrance gate and the covered tower opposite the north-west corner of the keep) was roofed. But all were originally two-storeyed and the holes made for the beams that supported the wooden floors can still be seen. The archers firing from the upper parapet were protected by wooden shutters, which have been restored. Each turret also contains two latrines discharging into the moat; these drain holes, which no doubt could have been used as machicolations during a siege, have all been sealed over except in the covered tower, where the stone seats have been left.

After the walls, the most remarkable external work is the gatehouse, which juts out some sixty feet from the line of the enceinte. The great outer door is defended by two machicolated towers; the attackers would also have had to face fire from loopholes in the side walls of the gatehouse. The whole structure, which is almost a castle in miniature, was designed to protect the main door in the curtain wall. If the attackers succeeded in forcing the outer gate, they had to run the gauntlet of two sets of machicolations—one at each end of the chapel above the passage. But in spite of these defences, the gatehouse at Ghent does not seem particularly formidable compared with the elaborate bent entrance at Krak and other crusader castles or the complex sequence of drawbridges, gates and portcullises at Caernarvon. The rooms in the gatehouse were later used as a torture chamber and as a prison, but the long room above the entrance passage must (as we have already assumed) originally have been the chapel; its design, the arcaded pillars and the cross-shaped window and arches at the end all support this interpretation. The shape of the window is most unusual, and may have been intended to symbolise the count's participation in the crusades.

The two main buildings inside the walls are the count's house and the keep; of these, the keep is the more important and dominates the whole castle and the surrounding city. Basically it comprises two great halls one above the other and linked by a ceremonial stair built in the thickness of the wall. The upper hall is the more

Above, a view of the great hall on the first floor of the keep taken from the arched entrance to the first-floor room (possibly a chapel) in the eastern wing adjoining the keep. The window seats are set in the thickness of the walls, as they are in the living quarters of many other castles.

Left, the chapel over the gatehouse. The blind arcading down the side walls recalls the chapel of Krak des Chevaliers and the cruciform window was, it has been suggested, a reminder of the count's participation in the Third Crusade.

impressive in its restored state; its huge size combined with a splendid fireplace and handsome rafters make it a fine example of medieval secular architecture. At the north end, a ramp-like structure rises from east to west; this is the covered staircase that led from the castellan's room (which is described later) to the turret stair up to the roof platform. The ground-floor hall rests on the walls and foundations of the original stone building, while the cellars below represent the first and second floors of this earlier castle. The new fabric was strengthened by additional pillars and vaulting. Adjoining the keep on its east and north sides are two buildings, which were probably later additions to the main structure. The one on the east, which has been fully restored, is remarkable for its handsome Romanesque windows; it comprises two rooms and two corner towers, of which the southern one contains a staircase. These two apartments may have been designed as the residence of the castellan; it is certainly unlikely, as has been suggested, that the upper room (which opens out into the main hall) was a chapel. The window-seats and fireplace are clear evidence of its domestic nature. The building on the north side of the keep probably housed the kitchens serving the two main halls.

The count's house, a residential building with the gabled front typical of town houses in Flanders, is situated to the west of the keep

Another view of the first-floor great hall of the keep showing the arched entrance to the adjoining wing and the ramp-like roofing of a staircase leading up from ground-floor level to the turret on the left. This interior staircase roofed with a stone vault and the arrow slit now looking into the hall (together with other structural features not visible in the picture) suggest that the hall originally stopped well short of the staircase, which would then have been outside the main building.

Above left, the handsome wing on the east of the central keep at the Gravensteen was added after the main structure had been built. The Romanesque windows on the first floor were probably those of the castellan's apartments; above may have been the chapel. In the foreground are the ventilation shafts to the subterranean stables. The shutters defending the embrasures are later reconstructions.

The plan of the Gravensteen can be seen in the aerial view, left, but note particularly the gatehouse, bottom left, which seems to be almost a separate castle.

and abuts on to the outer curtain wall. It was the official residence of the counts until the mid-14th century; it was then used to house law courts and legal offices. The audience chamber is particularly notable for its heavy vaulting supported by two free-standing columns and by corbels on the wall. Like other halls in the castle, it includes a noble fireplace. During the 14th century, the count's court of justice sat in the audience chamber, and in the adjoining room is a gruesome punishment cell, which, like the oubliettes of castles such as Conway, is entered by a trap-door in the ceiling. This underground pit is about 18 feet deep, with an area of 14 by 18 feet; it was a dank, cold prison with (needless to say) no sanitation, and ventilated only by a narrow winding chimney, which cut out all daylight. Some prisoners were confined here for as long as a year.

This prison was used until the 18th century; the torture instruments on display in the count's house, though similar to those used during the middle ages, are mostly from a later period and were in use up to the end of the 19th century. We have already seen that in the later history of the castle the chapel over the gatehouse was used as a torture chamber and prison; so too were the great subterranean stables by the east wall of the castle. The stables' magnificent vaulted ceiling, pierced by air shafts whose outlets can be seen from the wall-walk, is supported by eight central pillars; the roof was laid out as an exercise yard for prisoners during the 16th century.

In spite of its imposing appearance, the castle at Ghent was twice taken by storm during the 14th century. During this time, the ancient nobility of Europe was still posturing in the attitudes of a fashionable but outmoded chivalry, while its influence was being increasingly challenged by the growing wealth and power of the bourgeoisie. The second of these assaults, in 1338, was led by Jacques van Artevelde, the great patrician statesman of Ghent, who for four years successfully controlled the city against the count Louis of Nevers.

During the next century, when Ghent was ruled by the powerful dukes of Burgundy, the castle was used for administration and occasionally for court pageantry. The most magnificent of these displays was the meeting of the seventh chapter of the chivalric Order of the Golden Fleece. The order was founded by Duke Philip the Good (who probably modelled it on the English Order of the Garter) as part of his campaign for transforming his court into the most brilliant in Europe. Olivier de la Marche attended the chapter as a page and he has left us a full description. It is a vivid picture of

Opposite, interior of the Audience Chamber in the count's house. The small deeply set windows emphasise the military character of the castle whereas the massive fireplace, the fine vaulting and typically Gothic capitals of the supporting pillars reflect the grandeur of the aristocrats who lived there.

Below, Duke Philip the Good of Burgundy (1419–67). His reign consolidated the power of his house in the Low Countries where he inherited, among other things, the lands of the Counts of Flanders. Around his neck he wears the chain of the chivalric Order of the Golden Fleece, which was founded by him and which held its seventh chapter in the castle at Ghent.

the last stages of the flamboyant chivalry that was so popular with the 15th-century nobility and yet so out of place in the new society of towns and townsmen. The following extracts relate to the events at the Gravensteen.

'On Tuesday the sixth day of November, at about two o'clock in the afternoon, all the knights assembled in a council chamber [the audience chamber] of the castle, which had been furnished with seats and desks for their future deliberations. From here they went to the great hall [probably the ground-floor hall] which was thronged with lords and nobles; first came the three chief officers of the order clad in long scarlet robes, scarlet cloaks trimmed with grey fur, and scarlet hoods.

'After them came the knights, also in scarlet, and wearing a golden collar of muskets belching flames from which hung the noble Toison d'Or [the Golden Fleece, insignia of the order]; the edge of their cloaks was embroidered with the same design. The knights walked two by two, the most recently elected in the van the older knights at the rear, so that they were closer to the good Duke of Burgundy, the head and founder of this illustrious order. He walked alone behind his brethren, preceded by two sergeants at arms bearing pennants. To maintain the solemn precedence of the order, the duke even made his son, the Count of Charolais, most recently elected, walk at the front and therefore furthest from his father.'

After the mass on the second day there was a dinner, which Olivier also describes. It was held in the great hall of the castle, and in the background we can imagine not the bare stone walls of the present building but the richly coloured tapestries of Arras. 'The great table was covered with black velvet, richly embroidered with the arms and device of the Duke of Burgundy. On the left-hand side was a lower table for the accommodation of the officers of the Fleece. The wines and meats were plentiful and of the choicest, and the dinner lasted a long time, accompanied by the music of viols and trumpets and the cries of "largesse" from the heralds, who received great gifts from the knights. When the tables were raised, spices and wines were brought to the knights and princes, after which they retired to their apartments.'

The chivalric pomp and finery of this great feast in the castle at Ghent is a fitting end to our story, which began beneath the great walls of the White Tower in London. Built first for the austere purposes of war, the castles of Europe provided the stage for the elaborate theatricals of a later age.

Further reading list

Asche, Siegfried, *Die Wartburg*; Berlin, 1962
Edwards, J. G., *Edward I's Castle Building in Wales*; Oxford, 1944
Fedden, H. R. and Thomson, P., *Crusader Castles*; London, 1957
Harvey, John, *English Medieval Architects*; London, 1954
Torres Balbas, *Ars Hispaniae*, Vol. 4; Madrid, 1949
Smail, R. C., *Crusading Warfare*; Cambridge, 1956
Toy, Sidney, *A History of Fortification*; London, 1955

Glossary

arrow loops: slits in the walls of a fortress through which the bowmen of the garrison fired.

bailey: the area enclosed within a curtain wall or palisade; in it would be built outbuildings such as stables and kitchens.

balista: medieval artillery weapon operating on the principle of a giant crossbow.

barbican: masonry outwork built to protect the approach to a castle gate.

batter: the widening of the lower part of an outward facing wall or tower in a sharp or gentle upward slope. This widening of a wall at its base made it less vulnerable to sapping.

belfry: a fortified tower or movable siege-tower, which could be wheeled up to the wall of a castle so that the attackers could fire down on the besieged. It is thought to derive (like the German *Berchfrit*) from a Teutonic word meaning 'place of shelter'.

berquil: large outdoor reservoir found in crusader and Arab castles.

casemate: vaulted chamber built in the thickness of the castle ramparts.

castellan: the official commanding officer and governor of a castle.

cat: a roofed shelter on wheels to protect attackers approaching the walls of a castle from the missiles of the defending soldiers.

concentric castle: a central fortress ringed by a series of outer curtain walls.

curtain wall: main outer defensive wall of a castle's fortifications; it may be protected by towers and turrets but is not itself the wall of a building.

donjon: the correct term for the main tower or keep of a castle.

embrasure: another word for arrow loop.

enceinte: the entire circuit of a curtain wall.

glacis: a very pronounced outward-sloping masonry projection built out from the foot of a castle wall to protect it from sappers and miners.

keep: the main tower or stronghold of many castles, more correctly called a donjon.

machicolation: a stone projection on top of a castle wall with floor holes through which missiles could be dropped.

mangonel: a mechanical sling hurling missiles on a low trajectory.

merlon: the rising masonry wall on a battlement.

motte-and-bailey castle: the name given to a type of castle widespread in Normandy and England during the 10th and 11th centuries. In its simplest form, it consisted of a wooden fort on a hillock (either natural or artificial) called the motte, surrounded by a palisade enclosing the bailey.

pavise: heavy wooden shield used by crossbowmen to shelter behind when loading and firing.

petrariae: general term for medieval artillery weapons.

portcullis: iron-shod wooden grill moving vertically in grooved channels and used as additional protection to the gateway of a castle.

talus: a masonry projection to protect the base of a wall, similar to a glacis.

trebuchet: a mechanical sling hurling missiles on a high trajectory.

ward: an area of a castle's defences.

187

Index

Figures in italics refer to illustrations

Acknowledgements

Key to picture positions: (*T*) top, (*B*) bottom, (*L*) left, (*R*) right. Numbers refer to the pages on which the pictures appear.

Aerofilms 67, 69, 71, 87; Airviews (Man-chester) Ltd. 113(*B*); Alinari 59; Dr Sieg-fried Asche 174(*T*); Lala Aufsberg 20, 21, 25, 34, 35, 42, 66, 136, 151, 153(*L*), 153(*R*); Bavaria Verlag 156(*L*), 157, 169; Bayerische Staatsgemäldesammlungen 171(*T*); Alte Pinakothek, Munich 38; Belgian National Tourist Office 179, 184(*B*); Beringer and Pampaluchi Verlag 4, 160(*B*), 163, 165, 166(*C*), 166(*BL*), 167, 168; Bild-archiv Foto Marburg 95, 137(*T*), 178, 184(*TL*); Bodleian Library, Oxford 27(*B*), 48(*T*), 48(*B*), 49(*TL*); E. Boudot-Lamotte 103, 132, 138(*B*), 139, 142(*B*), 144(*B*), 154, 155(*L*), 155(*R*), 156(*R*); British Museum, London 15, 16, 22, 24(*T*), 26, 27(*T*), 28, 31, 32, 41, 49(*TR*), 51(*BR*), 53, 73, 117, 175(*R*); Camera Press 43(*T*); J. Allan Cash 111(*B*), 141, 143; Compagnie Aerienne Française 124(*B*), 125; J. E. Dayton 162, 166(*BR*);

Deutschereise Büro 177; French Govern-ment Tourist Office 102(*B*); Gianni Berengo Gardin 150; Paul Hamlyn Library 37; Her Majesty's Stationery Office 74(*TR*), 74(*TL*); Michael Holford 23, 57, 58, 60, 61, 64, 104(*T*), 104(*B*), 106, 107, 108(*T*), 108(*C*), 108(*B*), 109(*L*), 123(*T*), 120, 127, 128, 129; Heinemann Educational Books Ltd. 97, 123; Institut Belge d'Information et de Documentation 182(*T*), 182(*B*), 183, 184(*TR*); Italian State Tourist Office 109(*R*); A. F. Kersting 11, 12(*T*), 19, 36(*B*), 43(*B*), 55, 90, 91, 92, 93, 94(*L*), 94(*R*), 96–7, 97, 98, 99, 100, 102(*T*), 110–11, 112; Mansell Collection 39, 47, 52(*T*); Mansell/Alinari endpapers, 48–9; Mansell/Giraudon 185; Mas, Ampliaciones y Reproducciones 134(*T*), 142(*T*); Ministry of Public Building and Works 12(*B*), 46(*B*), 62, 68, 75(*L*), 75(*R*), 77, 79, 114(*B*), 115, 118(*T*), 118(*B*);

Musée Condé, Chantilly/Giraudon 17(*L*), 17(*R*); Museo Nazionale Florence/Mansell/Brogi 44; Hugh Newbury 81; Van Phillips, Feature Pix 133; Picturepoint Ltd. 51(*T*), 83(*B*), 84(*T*), 84(*B*), 85, 88, 114(*T*), 131, 135, 137(*B*), 138(*TR*), 144(*T*), 145(*T*), 145(*B*), 147, 148, 149; Pierpont Morgan Library, New York 30, 51(*BL*), 54; Willem van de Poll 14; Paul Popper Ltd. 36(*T*), 63, 76, 78, 83(*TL*), 83(*TR*), 86, 138(*TL*), 152; 164, 171(*B*); H. Roger-Viollet 10; Jean Roubier 13; Swiss National Tourist Office 160(*T*); Trinity College, Cambridge 33, 52(*B*); the Board of Trinity College, Dublin 24(*B*); Ullstein Bilderdienst 46(*T*), 170; Weiss, Agence Rapho 124(*T*); Walter Wolff (from the collection of Dr Asche) 172, 173(*T*), 173(*B*), 174(*B*), 175(*L*), 176; Zentrale Farbbild Agentur 180.